"Debbie is the real deal! Her story of God's blessings, joy and peace will inspire you! Through the trials of illness, hospital stays, surgeries and tough times, Debbie's spirit soars with smiles and ongoing praise to God! This lady is a solid, God honoring, Christian woman."

~ Rev. Cliff Bunch
Senior Pastor
First Baptist Church, Greensburg, Indiana

"Debbie Thomas exemplifies a life of courage and trust. Her life story will make you realize that God is still capable of parting the waters, slaying giants, turning water into wine and healing the sick. She has a heart of worship and it's all about Him! Get ready to be blessed!"

~ Brian Poling

"Our family has known Deb for nearly 15 years. It is not an exaggeration to say she is a walking miracle. We have observed her pilgrimage as she has labored through the valleys, and as well, scaled the mountaintop heights. Each and every step has been as a true follower of Christ – an authentic individual who has stayed the course through tremendous struggle, challenge and adversity. She has touched and inspired numerous lives with her indomitable spirit and reliance on Christ. As Paul wrote to the Philippians, Deb is a 'shining star in the universe as she holds out the word of life.' Several years ago, my wife and I suggested she write a book to share her incredible life events with others. You will be moved as you read her personal journey. You will discover a down-to-earth person who exudes genuine authenticity as she shares her trials of fear and discouragement, yet finding an unwavering refuge and hope in Christ. Deb Thomas has so richly blessed my life and you will be truly blessed as you read her story. You will soon discover, 'For Deb to live is Christ, and to die is gain'."

~ Rev. David B. Thompson
Associate Pastor
First Baptist Church, Greensburg, Indiana

FROM
PAIN
TO
JOY in the midst
of suffering

peace

DEBBIE J. THOMAS

WINTERS
PUBLISHING
winterspublishing.com
812-663-4948

From Pain to Peace - JOY in the Midst of Suffering

© 2011 Debbie J. Thomas

Published by:
Winters Publishing
P.O. Box 501
Greensburg, IN 47240
812-663-4948
www.winterspublishing.com

Cover design by Rachel Winters

ISBN 10: 1-883651-48-4
ISBN 13: 978-1-883651-48-0

Library of Congress Control Number: 2011938496

Printed in the United States of America

Dedication

This book is dedicated to my loving husband, Larry,
and our two children, Sam and Megan.

You have been an encouragement and support
throughout the years, but never has your love for me
been more evident than in the past six years.
The past six years were an incredible struggle
for our entire family, but we supported one another
and relied on God to pull us through.
I could not have made it through these
difficult years without God and you!
I thank God for His work in all our lives and
for the wonderful family He has blessed me with!

Thank you for taking such good care of me
and for loving me as you do.
I love you more than you'll ever know.

~ Debbie ... Mom

Acknowledgments

In telling my story, I was extremely fortunate to work with a very dedicated professional and two very special family members. I have been most impressed with their dedication, but ultimately I have been overjoyed by their character and love for me.

George Granholt has invested an enormous amount of time into the making of this book. He has encouraged me, and kept me sane as he guided me through the long and delicate editing process. George's professional "eye" and expertise have been invaluable to me, and I have been blessed to learn so much from the wonderful experience of writing this book. He has become an unexpected treasure to me and one I will never forget.

Mary Wilkinson is also an author, but first and foremost, she is my sister. She has been my ultimate cheerleader and mentor. She has prayed for me, encouraged me, and cautioned me in every phase of the creation of this book. She offered tips and techniques that proved to be extremely helpful and even helped me name the book. Mary also spent countless hours editing my book in its initial stages – a true labor of love. Without her enormous efforts and sensitive spirit, *From Pain to Peace - JOY in the Midst of Suffering* would not be the book it is today.

Finally, Sherry Stoneking is also my sister, and she has also been a huge encouragement to me. She did some editing for me, but most importantly, she and her small group from church prayed for me continually. They will never know how much those prayers meant to me, and how their prayers carried me through the entire process of the development of the book.

Special thanks to MainSource for their help in making this book a reality.

I thank God for each person He put in my life to help me tell my story. I count it a privilege and blessing to have such special friends and an incredible family. It is because of God and God alone, that I tell my story, and God should receive all the glory, honor and praise!

Contents

Foreword

(Written by my son – Samuel Ray Thomas)

Many people who are skeptical about there being a God have asked the age old question, "If God is so perfect and so loving, why does He let such terrible hardships happen to good people?"

This is the question I cried out to God on the day my mother was experiencing the most horrific pain of all her operations. After hearing the screams come from the hospital room for a couple of minutes, I ran to a secluded bathroom to cry out to God, asking Him, "Why her, why not me? I deserve this, she doesn't!"

I asked this in the midst of a flood of tears and a lot of anger. The answer God gave me was one that I didn't fully understand until later.

He answered, "Because I love you."

At the time of the bulk of her operations, I was questioning my beliefs about God, religion, and certain moralities. I was also running from what I know today is the truth. That truth, taught since I was a young child, was simply that God is love. The purpose of our life is to reflect His character in such a way that others want to develop a relationship with Him. I didn't want to accept this as fact because meeting God's requirement was contradictory to my personality.

I am what I call a "people pleaser." This individual is one who seeks approval from others to avoid conflict or pain. The root of this kind of personality is insecurity about one's self. It is a gift from God, but it becomes a curse if there is no sacrifice to Him daily. The desire to have everyone like me has paid dividends in my career and other parts of my life, but it severely hurt my relationship with God. It was through numerous, deep conversations by my mother's hospital bed that I found out she suffered from the same personality issues.

What was most difficult for me to understand was that my mom viewed all of her surgeries and disabilities as a way of intervention from a life of half-hearted commitment to God. I was astounded that she had that kind of perspective on her life. She was stripped of her dignity, security, independence, and some of the most basic aspects of life we take for granted, yet in all of this, she praised God.

The first lesson she taught me, through all of this, was that when she lost control of her life and had to fully rely on God, she experienced a joy and peace that was foreign to me. After seeing her inspire so many people through her life story and witnessing the unexplainable miracles that puzzled her doctors, my mother's disability made Christianity real to me. Her story was the proof I needed, and I saw it as one of the reasons God allowed her to endure those terrible conditions.

I owe my mother more than I will ever be able to repay. If it were not for all of her serious health conditions, I am not sure I would be the Christian and the man that I am today. I still struggle with my insecurity, but because of our deep talks on many long nights at her bedside, I understand the psychology of why I have such a commitment problem to God, but find it easy to commit to people. The understanding of my emotions and my actions has helped me make huge strides in my commitment to Christ.

The journey I have been on with her, and still continue, has shown me that God uses people's pain to bring more glory to Himself, so that skeptical people like me can't deny His love. This is why I can say with complete confidence that God is a jealous God and wants very much to be in relationship with us. He will go as far as letting someone we love dearly endure unjust circumstances if that is what it takes to bring us to our knees.

My mother is more than a parent to me; she is my hero. If it were not for her pain, I would not have found my purpose in life. I am convinced that if God would have given me another mother, I never would have been able to control my emotional issues and would be in jail or dead by now. I cannot thank her enough for being the example I needed to help me realize Christianity is not just a religion. It is a relationship which provides freedom.

My prayer is that as you read her story, God will reveal Himself to you in a new and vivid way and that it will inspire you, as it did me, to start living a life that seeks God's approval and no longer needs validation from others.

Introduction

This book is a true story that helps answer the age old question of why serious adversities happen to good people. My testimony is proof that God will allow intense pain and incredible hardships in a person's life if it means others will come to know Him through that person's pain and, in the process, He will be glorified. I chose to write this story not as a simple narrative, but rather a parallel to the Book of Job. Job and I, as well as countless others, share what many Christians have in common. We have endured pain, suffering, and hardships that we did not deserve, nor did we think we could handle.

Through these hardships people ask, "Where does the joy come from in the midst of your circumstances?", "How do you smile when your life has robbed you of your independence?" and "Why aren't you mad at God? He allowed this!"

My prayer is that through my testimony, God will enlighten anyone reading this with these answers, as He has enlightened me.

The Book of Job, as well as all Scripture, is inspired of God. Though the Book of Job is thousands of years old, God is still revealing truths to us today. We can all learn much from Job. The Book of Job is a testament of how everyone can overcome and have victory even in the absolute darkest of times. Although we will most likely never experience the torment and losses Job experienced, we should take notice of Job's deep love and devotion for God. As we find ourselves in a crisis, I pray we will exude the qualities of Job. I pray that we can still glorify God no matter how hideous our circumstances may be.

Chapter 1

A Glimpse of Heaven
(January 8, 2006, I.U. Medical Center)

Then something incredible happened. All the noise and chatter ceased. I was in a completely different place – far away. Instantly, the excruciating pain was gone – completely gone! "What on earth just happened?" I wondered. "This is crazy!" I had no idea what was happening or where I was. My mind was spinning, and I tried to get a grasp of what was actually going on.

Then I saw myself standing in a place of brilliant light. It was the brightest pure white light imaginable. I could barely open my eyes because the light was so intense, and there was nowhere to look that the light didn't shine so brilliantly.

I heard trumpets, horns and violins. I could hear singing, but I could not make out the words of the song, however, I knew it was praise: praises to God. I heard birds chirping. I could hear them so clearly, even above all the music, but I could not see them. Children laughed and played. I heard little girls giggle and squeal. They were having so much fun, and it was so refreshing. Although I could not see them, I knew they were playing chase, and several children were holding hands circled all around the Tree of Life. The laughter was contagious. I couldn't help but smile. What was this place? Was it heaven, I wondered? It was so peaceful and unlike any place I had ever known. I wanted so badly to discover its source, but I could not. Then I heard a voice, a male voice. I knew instantly it was Jesus. My heart swelled and I feared it would burst.

"Today, you are coming home."

I looked for the source of the voice, but no one was there. I turned every direction and tried to stare into what I thought was the most brilliant source of light. Still, I could see nothing, and I could barely speak.

"God," I asked, "am I coming home today?"

No answer. I felt a wave of sweet relief come over me and a soothing peace I'd never felt before. I had absolutely no fear. The thought of being in heaven and being out of all the misery and pain was such a welcome relief. I waited for what seemed like several minutes and asked, "God, please let me die in surgery so that I don't linger and have to be in any more pain, and so my family will not have to suffer with this any longer."

Again, there was no response. I just stood there frozen in time, lingering in the light and the laughter of the children. Paralyzed with wonder and amazement, I wanted to see and hear more, but that was not to be. What a gift to be given: a glimpse of heaven. Never again will I fear death, and I look forward to heaven and all that awaits me there. I am excited and so thankful that I have the promise of eternal life in Christ. I remember feeling so grateful for this brief moment in time of the complete absence of pain and sorrow! What an awesome God we serve!

Chapter 2

Job: Blameless and Upright

Job was a man depicted in the Holy Bible as one who was found blameless and upright. He feared God and shunned evil. He had seven sons and three daughters; he owned seven thousand sheep, three thousand camels, five hundred yoke of oxen and five hundred donkeys. He had a large number of servants, and he was considered the greatest man among all the people of the East.

One day the angels came to present themselves before the LORD, and Satan also came with them. The LORD said to Satan, "Where have you come from?"

Satan answered the LORD, "From roaming through the earth and going back and forth in it."

Then the LORD said to Satan, "Have you considered my servant Job? There is no one on earth like him; he is blameless and upright, a man who fears God and shuns evil."

"Does Job fear God for nothing?" Satan replied. "Have you not put a hedge around him and his household and everything he has? You have blessed the work of his hands, so that his flocks and herds are spread throughout the land. But stretch out your hand and strike everything he has, and he will surely curse you to your face."

The LORD said to Satan, "Very well, then, everything he has is in your hands, but on the man himself do not lay a finger" (Job 1:6-12).

Then as Job's sons and daughters feasted and drank wine at a brother's house, Job got a message. The oxen and donkeys were carried off by the Sabeans. All the servants were killed except for the one who brought the message to Job. Fire burned up all the sheep and the Chaldeans carried off all his camels. Finally, the servant told Job that all of his sons and daughters were killed when the wind "swept up and struck the four corners of the house." It collapsed on them. In the blink of an eye, Job lost all that he worked for: his possessions and his family. How much could one man take?

At this, Job got up and tore his robe and shaved his head. Then he fell to the ground in worship and said: "Naked I came from my mother's womb, and naked I will depart. The LORD gave and the LORD has taken away; may the name of the LORD be praised." In all this, Job did not sin by charging God with wrongdoing (Job 1:20-22).

Worship? Really? Who is this Job who can remain faithful under all that he has endured? As did Job, I have been and continue to be tested. Believe me, I am no saint and I understand God has a lot of work to do in me and through me. I, too, have wondered why this is happening to me.

I've asked God, "If I have some unconfessed sin, or have done something wrong that I am not aware of, please tell me what it is so I can confess it and seek forgiveness." Sometimes, God does bring to mind something that I need to deal with, but other times, I don't have a clue.

I ask, "Why has God allowed Satan to attack me on all fronts? Why has my suffering been allowed to go on for so long?" I am tired, I'm weak and I'm an emotional train wreck. I have learned many times over to just trust. So, I will. I am trusting that God will take care of this, and that He has my back and that good will come of it. In all of my troubles, I pray that my words and actions will glorify Him. I don't know the reason for all God's ways, but I do know that His ways are right and just. He has big plans for me!

"For I know the plans I have for you," declares the LORD, "plans to prosper you and not to harm you, plans to give you hope and a future" (Jeremiah 29:11).

Chapter 3

What Was I Thinking? (Mid October 1982, Home)

Shortly after Larry and I were married, we attended a little Southern Baptist Church in Batesville, Indiana. The church was holding a revival, and I had never been to one. I had no clue what it was, and I was rather curious, so we went. It was like nothing I had ever expected or experienced. I was raised Catholic, so it was definitely an eye opener for me. People were shouting, "Amen, preach it, brother!" and all kinds of odd remarks while the preacher gave his message!

It was very distracting and honestly quite rude, I thought. I wondered if these people knew how to behave in church. I grew up believing the congregation should be quiet and respectful in church. As uncomfortable as I felt with the service, I didn't want to leave just yet. I was intrigued and the minister was very engaging. He walked up and down the aisles, seeming as if he was talking to us and not at us. Something drew me in, and I hung on to every word the man was saying.

Then he changed his message as he began speaking about salvation. I was feeling a little sick to my stomach by then; it must have been over one hundred degrees in that room, because I sweated profusely. The church was packed, and I wondered if that was one reason it was so warm. I also thought I might be coming down with the flu. The minister went on to explain how we could accept Jesus as our personal Lord and Savior.

I had heard this message before, and I already believed in God. I thought now might be a good time to slip out since I was feeling so poorly. I turned to Larry and whispered that I was ready to leave. Of course, he wanted to stay. Great! I sat back and tried to pull myself together. There was no easy way to step over everyone in the pew to slip out without being noticed. I was trapped! As I listened, I heard something a little different that night from what I heard before. The minister said Jesus is the only way to God.

"It's not good enough just to believe in God," he said. "Even the devil believes in God."

Suddenly it hit me. I truly believed in God, but I never realized that I needed a personal relationship with Jesus. I had God in my head, but I didn't have Jesus in my heart! Then the minister began talking about the Tylenol scare of 1982 that gripped the United States. He pressed the point that there is no guarantee of tomorrow. All we have is this moment in time – right here, right now. Some heinous criminal tampered with Tylenol products, and people were being poisoned and dying.

The preacher kept repeating over and over, "We have no guarantee of tomorrow. What if you had taken one of those poisoned Tylenols? What if you walk out these doors and keel over dead? Where would you be? Are you sure you would go to heaven?"

He fired questions left and right. With each query my heart pounded harder and harder. My fingertips turned blue from the grip I had on the pew in front of me, and I was so convicted I could hardly breathe. I needed out of there in the very worst way! I knew I needed Jesus in my heart and as my Lord and Savior, but I had a BIG problem!

We'd only been attending this church a short time when I was asked to teach the children's Sunday School class, and I agreed. Here I was teaching a Sunday School class, and I was not even saved myself! My feet shifted back and forth and I felt completely overwhelmed. If I went forward and admitted that I had not fully understood my need for Jesus, these people would eat me alive! How on earth would they ever forgive me? I kept hearing, "Keep your mouth shut!" Satan was working overtime trying to prevent me from making a move. I wanted to run as fast as I could and as far away from there as I could possibly get! By this time, I was ready to vomit! Then it happened. I could not hold back. I lost my grip on the pew.

"Wait a minute! I'm not ready!"

It felt as if someone pulled me from my pew and pushed me up the aisle. I would be crucified! What was I thinking? Before

I knew it, I was up front sobbing, and it was over. They all knew now, and I didn't care anymore. The fear left me, and I decided it was time to confess, no matter what the consequence might be. I needed peace and I really wanted a relationship with Jesus. I was ready to make my personal profession of faith, and I knelt with the minister and prayed the sinner's prayer. I accepted Jesus Christ as my personal Lord and Savior, and I was elated! Wow, what a relief! There were no lightning bolts, no crashing of thunder or any other earth shattering experience – just an overwhelming release of control, the weight off my shoulders, and the feeling of pure joy and delight. All those thoughts of condemnation were gone. Not a single person in that room condemned me; instead, I was greeted with incredible love and understanding.

As I have grown in my faith, I have come to love and trust Jesus more and more. My faith and relationship with Jesus have been tested many times. At times in my life I have been confused about everyday problems and struggles with testing. I know I am going to have troubles in my life no matter how weak or strong my faith is. This world is full of sin, and I am living smack dab in the middle of it. I can't escape it, and most of the time I cause my own problems. That doesn't necessarily mean that every problem is a test. Yes, God does test us at times because He wants to push us and encourage us to reach our full potential. Our ultimate goal is to be Christ-like, as that is the literal meaning of "Christian."

I started out as a baby Christian and I've been working on maturing in Christ ever since. I am Jesus' adopted daughter, and people should be able to see a resemblance of my Father, Jesus, in me. Jesus wanted a relationship with me, and He was willing to take me just the way I was. He understood what a mess I was and that was okay with Him; He loved me in spite of all my faults and failures. So, being the intelligent person I am, I accepted. I know a good deal when I see it! What's even more amazing is that He loves me so much that when I finally did come to Him, He was not willing to let me stay as I was. He knows my potential and He wants the very best for me! So, He's continually working in me in ways I never dreamed possible, and He allows challenges to happen in my life that will help me to develop a Christ-like mind-set.

It's no different from the way we raise our own children. We allow them to work out problems on their own so they can learn valuable life lessons and Christian values we wish to instill in them. All this learning and development is not necessarily a result of testing. It's just living our life, and the growth comes from how we respond to our circumstances.

As I have grown in my relationship with Christ and I have become more Christ-like, I realize that I am more prone to testing. Testing is the practice for perfection. I know I won't be perfect or sinless until I am in heaven with Jesus. As long as I'm here on earth, I will continue to sin, but my goal is to avoid the sin and strive to be more like Jesus. Testing is the opportunity to use the lessons I've learned to bring results that show me to be "upright and blameless," just as Job was when tested. It demonstrates my desire and effort to come out of my testing as one who truly reflects the image of Christ. I want to be my "Daddy's girl."

There is not one single event that happens in my life that God won't use to strengthen my faith and to bring glory to Himself. Every adversity and trial I face helps to shape me and bring me closer to the image of Christ. My life has been far from a bowl of cherries, but it gets sweeter and sweeter the closer I get to my Jesus. I wouldn't have it any other way.

Chapter 4

Who Doesn't Have Problems?
(December 2005, Decatur County Memorial Hospital)

Yes, like everyone else on the face of this earth, I have problems. Sometimes I am overwhelmed with them. It seems I get one problem taken care of and along comes another. No one is exempt from tribulation. Some refer to their difficult circumstances as strife, adversities, struggles or trials. It's all the same, and we all have problems.

Job had problems as well. What helped Job to develop and strengthen his faith in God was the way he chose to deal with his issues. He did not allow his adversities to become a stumbling block in his relationship with God. I have a choice to make every time I am confronted with a difficult situation. I can take matters into my own hands and hope for the best, or I can give my struggles to God, and allow Him to guide me through it. Job took his troubles to God. I know this because Job feared God. He was upright and blameless, and he was emulating Christ-like qualities; a true testament of his character. The qualities that he developed, as a result of his dealings with previous problems, helped him face and overcome his greatest test of all.

Satan was not happy with Job and was sure he could cause Job to fall. He wanted the chance to prove it. Satan banked on proving that Job was righteous only because "it profited him." If Satan proved this to be the case, he would win his bet with the Lord.

"Oh, the sweet taste of victory!" Satan drooled at the thought of his win.

Even Job's friends railed against him. They were wise and understood biblical truths, they believed in God's ultimate authority, that God is just in His dealings, and that no one is completely sinless. They believed the source of Job's problems was the result and

punishment of his sin. Satan hates Christians and tries relentlessly
to drive a wedge between God and His beloved. The attacks from
Satan are the "problems" that become a test of our loyalty and love
for Jesus Christ. In Job's case, his problems were definitely a test.
For me, sometimes it is about testing and sometimes it's not. I
believe God is doing a lot of character building in me. He's teaching
me humility and so much more.

It all started when I woke up on December 17th, 2005. I went
to work as I did any other day. I was not feeling the best and
assumed I was coming down with the flu, but I needed to go to
work. Mondays were extremely busy. I usually do my best work
when I am under pressure, but this particular day I was completely
overwhelmed. I felt very warm, and I was very nauseated and on
the verge of tears. I had no idea how I would make it through the
day, but I just knew I needed to be at work. I practically fell into
my chair, and I knew I'd better start my day with prayer.

"God, I need help. I am sick, really sick, and I can't do this by
myself. Please help me to focus and make it through this day."

A couple of hours into my morning I was in bad shape. I knew
I had a fever and my face was as red as a beet. My stomach churned,
and I was sure I would vomit if I tried to move. Again, I went to
prayer.

"God, something is very wrong. If this is exhaustion, or stress,
give me a way to escape it. If not, help me to know the difference.
PLEASE, help me! I don't think I'm going to make it!"

My prayers became more desperate the worse I felt. By noon,
I was so ill I could barely drive home. I made it to the car, but
driving home was going to be an even bigger challenge. I started to
suffer with a migraine headache, and I could feel my blood pressure
rising.

Thump. Thump! Thump!! I thought my head would pound
off, and I could barely focus while driving home. Finally, I did make
it home, and I practically crawled to the bathroom. If I could just
get in the tub and soak in some hot water I might feel better. Bad
idea! I didn't realize the hot water could raise my blood pressure
even more, and the longer I sat in the tub the more afraid I became.
I wasn't sure if I could get out of the tub. I had the portable phone

by the tub and called my sister-in-law Deanna. It didn't take long for her to realize something was seriously wrong.

Within a matter of minutes she was at my door, and she loaded me into the car and headed to the hospital. We went straight to the ER, but it was well over a half hour before I was even taken back to a room. The wait was incredibly difficult as I sat on the hard plastic chair in the waiting room, because I could barely stay in an upright position. I gave the nurse my basic history, and she started to work me up for possible heart problems.

In August of 2005, I had suffered a heart attack, and the cardiologist discovered I had a left bundle branch blockage. I had a heart catheterization, and a stent was placed in one of my blocked arteries. I was told I should be fine, and if I took my medications as directed, I shouldn't have any more problems for awhile. They were right. I haven't had any heart symptoms or problems since. However, because of the prior heart history and my blood pressure, the ER doctor did an EKG and a slew of cardiac labs. The EKG did not reveal much, and it would take awhile to know the results of the blood work. My blood pressure soared and I vomited profusely. The ER doctor felt uncomfortable waiting for all the lab results to come back, so he immediately decided to have me transferred to a hospital in Indianapolis that specializes in cardiac care. I could see him pacing back and forth just outside my room as we waited for the ambulance.

The ambulance ride was fairly uneventful except for the fact that the driver raced at break-neck speeds, and the cot I was strapped to slid from side to side, similar to a carnival ride. I was already extremely nauseated, which only made matters worse. Fortunately, I didn't vomit while I was in the ambulance, but there were a few times I thought I would. The sirens blared the entire way to the hospital and, at one point, the throb in my head began to mimic the wail of the sirens.

"Are we there yet?" I couldn't wait to get out of that ambulance. I honestly did not understand at the time just how serious my condition was. I knew I was sick but, my goodness, what was the emergency!

When I got to the hospital in Indianapolis, I was rushed to

a room where several nurses waited to hook me up to all sorts of monitors and devices. Wires tangled, needles flew, and I felt really anxious. The EMT gave me another dose of anti-nausea medicine, but the excruciating dry heaves just kept coming. I clutched my stomach and rolled from side to side, but I still could not get any relief. The doctor could not understand why I continued to vomit so copiously. The EKG was abnormal, but there was no sign of a heart attack and that was good news. Still, my blood pressure was extremely high and I was dehydrated. I asked the cardiologist if the problem could be my stomach, but he didn't feel that was the source of the problem. He put me through a battery of heart tests, blood work, and X-rays, but none really confirmed any heart related problems. After four days of extensive testing, the cardiologist confirmed what I already knew: my problem was not heart-related.

Because of the continued vomiting, the cardiologist decided my problem might be gastrointestinal. I remember suggesting that on more than one occasion, but I was not the doctor, and he let me know it. The hospital's CAT scanner was down so the doctor transferred me to another hospital, which was less than a half mile away, to have the abdominal scan. The CAT scan revealed I had a bowel obstruction.

Finally, we had an answer. I had a third bowel obstruction and I was devastated! I was diagnosed with severe endometriosis in the early 1990's, which resulted in massive adhesions growing in my abdomen. In 1995 I developed my first bowel obstruction caused by those severe adhesions. In 2000 I had a second bowel obstruction, also caused by adhesions. Now, nearly five years later, in December of 2005, the doctor discovered this third bowel obstruction, and I would undergo another surgery! I was beside myself, as there seemed to be a pattern developing of a bowel obstruction every five years. What was going on?

My husband, Larry, and I prayed about the surgery, but I still did not have a good feeling about the bowel obstruction or the surgery. The surgeon came in and answered all our questions, and we were a little more at ease. I wondered why all this was happening to me.

"Hadn't I been through enough? Lord, You promised not to

give me more than I could bear. I'm just wondering if You are aware of what's going on here."

As the thought came to my mind, so did the words of Christ, *"… O you of little faith?" (Matthew 6:30).* Ouch! I knew better. God is so faithful and He has ALWAYS been with me. I asked God to take away my fear and to let me make it through the surgery without any problems.

"What I feared has come upon me; what I dreaded has happened to me. I have no peace, no quietness; I have no rest, but only turmoil" (Job 3:25-26).

Job lost everything. He did not understand, and He asked God a barrage of questions. Why, why, why? He had no answer from God. Groaning day and night, Job could find no relief, yet, he did not sin against God.

Faith is very difficult at times. I know my love for God, but still, I question Him at times. As Job, I have asked why. How I must disappoint God at times. I cannot help but wonder why all these adversities come against me. I have no answer from God, but I trust in Him and praise Him.

The surgery went well, we thought. The surgeon told my family that he nicked my bowel in three places, but it should be okay. He had a very difficult time trying to free the bowel from other organs because of the widespread adhesions. He felt confident that he sealed all the leaks, and I should be fine. I did fairly well post-op: no fever or complications, and three days later, I was sent home.

I awoke at home a few days later with a very high fever and acute abdominal pain. I could barely stand up, much less walk. I didn't feel this way after my last bowel surgery, and I knew something was very wrong. I slowly made it to the kitchen and stopped at the end of the counter. I couldn't go any further, and thought I might pass out. Larry panicked! "Deb, you look really bad. I'm calling the doctor. Maybe we should go to the hospital."

"No, I'm fine. Just let me stand here a minute and I'll be okay. Get me my pain medicine." I did not want to go back to the hospital if I could help it.

I mumbled so badly I don't know how Larry understood what

I was asking for. I took the pain medicine and turned to head back to bed. Larry kept pressing me to go to the hospital, but I kept insisting I'd be okay. I tried to make it back to bed, but I couldn't get any further than the couch. Larry called my sister Anna for reinforcements, and in a matter of a few minutes she barged in, and the two of them loaded me into the car and rushed me to the ER.

Here we go again; hurry up and wait. The nurses were very nice and tried to help as much as they could, but we had to wait for a doctor. They put me in a room and we waited for what seemed like an eternity before a surgeon came in to check me out. My stomach was distended and I vomited again. The pain was unbearable, and the more I threw up, the worse the pain. The surgeon told us that my bowel was leaking, but it was New Year's Eve and he could not locate another surgeon to assist him in surgery. That was okay with me because I didn't want a surgeon who might have been out drinking and celebrating cutting on me! So, I was scheduled to have surgery the next day – New Year's Day. I don't remember much of the emergency room experience except that Anna never left my side. She was my advocate and she sat with me for hours as I vomited and cried out in pain.

Once I was finally moved to a regular room, everyone went home except for Larry and the children. I felt really discouraged that my family had not even celebrated Christmas yet. Megan and Sam weren't complaining, but the holidays were ruined, nonetheless. I could see the worry on all their faces, and Megan was the most concerned.

Megan and I both worked at the Medical Multi-Specialty Clinic, and we were well aware of how deadly a bowel obstruction can be if it ruptures. This leak was serious and she knew it. We said our prayers, and I kissed my family good night. For the first time in hours the room was silent. I had a long time to think about the situation, and what the outcome might be. I knew God was protecting me, or I would have been dead already. I wondered what His plan was, and I begged for Him to let me live so I could take care of my family. I couldn't get past the strong possibility that I may not survive the surgery. I had a lot of unfinished business.

Who would take care of the children? What about making

plans for college? I hadn't completed the FAFSA forms yet!
Larry didn't know where the bills were, and I'd never showed him
where I kept the life insurance policy and the important papers. I
had customers who were expecting calls from me at work. I had
new employees to train, and I had a training session with a client
in a couple of weeks! What a horrible time for all of this to be
happening!

I was so unsettled. The nurse came in with more medications,
and something she gave me made me very drowsy. I wrestled with
my worries for a few moments and finally began to feel a little more
at ease about the surgery. God showed me that He was in control,
and He knows what's best for me. It wasn't long before I was fast
asleep, but I didn't stay asleep.

"I have no peace, no quietness; I have no rest, but only turmoil"
(Job 3:26).

Job's words seem to paint a picture of just how I felt. I was
awake most of the night praying, because I needed God's assurance
that I would survive to care for my family. Sam and Meg were both
in the middle of some major transitions, and I felt it was my job, as
their mom, to help them through this time of uncertainty. I worried
about my children all the time. Okay, so I'm a little bit of a control
freak. Maybe I'm a big control freak, but I can't help it! I want my
children to have perfect lives, and in a perfect world my children
would go to the perfect school, get the perfect job, and have the
perfect life without all the struggles I had as a young adult.

Don't get me wrong. I didn't have horrible strife as a young
adult, but I did struggle, and I did have to work very hard to get
where I was. I was organized and structured, and I took my work,
any work, very seriously. I tried to give my very best in all situations;
work, play or life in general, and I've tried to instill these same
values in our children. Sam and Megan were well on their way to
being very independent young adults, but I found it extremely hard
to cut the apron strings. I knew God would understand, and I just
needed Him to give me a sign. That assurance did not come.

What did eventually come was a peace: a peace that He was
in control and whatever the outcome, His will would be done. That
was the same assurance I had felt the night before, but this time I

was satisfied. I didn't understand how, but I was satisfied, and I praised God and thanked Him for the time I'd been given. I was privileged to raise and nurture the most incredible children. They were healthy, smart, hard workers, and they had a firm foundation in their faith. They had both accepted Jesus as their personal Lord and Savior. That was the most important experience I prayed for my children, and my prayers were answered. For that, I praised God all the more.

Morning finally came. Bright and early the nurses came in to prep me for surgery. My family gathered around my bed and we prayed together. The mood was somber, and I tried to reassure them that I was going to be fine – as best I could.

By now, I had formed a wonderful relationship with the doctors, nurses, and even the cleaning staff at our local hospital, Decatur County Memorial Hospital. They were all so kind to me. They understood all that I'd been through, and I was so thankful for their compassion. God knew I needed the surgeon, the doctors and those nurses, and He prepared all of them for the task at hand.

Our prayers were answered … I made it through. The surgeon said my bowel was so thin it was like tissue paper. The surgery took over six hours, and halfway through the surgery he had to stop and call for additional assistance. He was fighting a losing battle with all the adhesions. The surgeon removed a large portion of my intestines and was very concerned that the repairs he made might not hold. He was careful not to give my family any false impressions that I was going to be okay, and he made sure they understood my intestines were in terrible shape, and it would be touch and go for awhile. He planned to keep me in the hospital until he was sure everything worked as it should. I was so weak I didn't care what they did at that point. So we waited and waited. Each day that followed brought new complications and more pain.

I was in intensive care for several days, but the first couple of days I was in excruciating pain. I remember my sister Tina was there. My son, Sam, was on one side of me, and Tina was on the other. I didn't feel like talking; I just wanted them there. A nurse suggested that Sam should go home and get some rest, because it was a very long day, but he refused to leave. Instead, Sam sat in that hard chair at the side of my bed and lay his head down beside me. I was so proud of him and thankful he stayed with me. I think he must have fallen asleep, because he was in that same position for a very long time. Tina stood on my left. I cried and begged for pain medicine, but I could not get any relief, and it was horrible. I drifted off to sleep, and since I couldn't push my pain button, I'd wake up hurting so bad it was unbearable! I asked Tina to please stay, and she did, and every time I woke up with the awful pain, Tina was there. She just stood there holding my hand; she was my angel, and I needed that so badly. I was so thankful for what she did for me. The next day, Tina was still there, and so was Sam; I couldn't believe it! They were such a welcome relief, and I was overwhelmed with gratitude that they stayed all night with me. I thanked them repeatedly.

After a couple of minutes, Tina said, "Deb, what are you talking about? I was here for a while, but I had to go home because the kids had school, and I couldn't stay. I wanted to stay, believe me, but I couldn't."

I was dumbfounded! What? I saw her – every time I looked up she was there, and she held my hand all night! What had God done? He allowed me the comfort of seeing her there with me even when she wasn't physically there. Her spirit was there and I saw it and felt it! What a wonderful and marvelous God we have!

I lost track of the days, and once I remember waking up in a totally different room. I didn't even remember the nurses moving me. I had my Bible, but I couldn't even focus, much less read, because I was on so much medication. I had a little book tucked inside my Bible called *God's Promises*, and it had a topical list of Scriptures in large print. I searched for Scriptures of God's promises for protection and healing. I held on to those promises. I needed Jesus more than ever to help me face all that would come against me, and He was there. When I got discouraged, He was there. He put wonderful people in my path to show me His mighty love and mercy. The entire hospital staff was incredible! Church members and friends came almost daily to visit. Co-workers, past and present, showed up to encourage and support me. And my family was always there for me.

I often wondered, when I read the book of Job, why God

gave Satan so much control over Job. Why did God allow so much infliction of pain and agony on Job, only to spare his life? Job lost everything and he wanted to die. In fact, he asked God why he did not perish at birth. He got no answer. It is ironic that Job's testing was not a test from God. It was a test from Satan! God allowed it, but it was Satan who was throwing the punches. God knows everything, and He already knew what the outcome would be for Job, so why allow such severe testing?

God knows my outcome, too. However, I don't know how I will measure up just yet. I have no intention of ever cursing God or being unfaithful to God, but my story isn't over yet. I'm human and I'm still on this journey.

There have been times when I wanted to die as well. I've questioned the reason I am even alive. I have declared my intent to trust God. It's up to me to honor God by following through with what I promised. It's always decision time, because we have free will. My reaction to my circumstances will testify to my love and honor for God. God knew what Job's response would be, but Job didn't know for sure what he would do until he actually stepped out to follow through and trust God. If Job or I knew the outcome of our challenges, we would certainly be firm in our faith, instead of wobbling back and forth at times. But then, that wouldn't be faith, would it? Nevertheless, Job remained faithful.

On January 8, 2006, I awoke in my hospital room at Decatur County Memorial Hospital, burning up with fever. I could tell my stomach was swollen and my covers were covered in thick, stinky goop. There was a terrible odor coming from the drainage. Instantly, I knew in my heart I was not going to make it.

"Lord, help me, please! Give me a way to cope. Help me hold it together a little longer so I can get help. I want to see Larry and my children before I die. Help me to clear my mind and understand what's going on here."

I pleaded with God to guide me through. I came to know that God is faithful in all circumstances and in all times, and this was no exception! I questioned my survival, but I did not question the fact that the process would be perfectly orchestrated according to His plan.

I needed to get my thoughts together to get help, and the medications had me in a fog. I called my husband and told him to come immediately. I don't even think I told him why. He knew by the terror in my voice that I needed him right now and not to wait. Then I called my sister Anna and told her to find the doctor. I knew she could "rattle some bones" and get people hopping, and that is exactly what I needed. Then I hit the call light. Anna lived about twelve minutes from the hospital and I don't even think she took time to brush her hair. She and Larry were there within a matter of minutes. It was 5:30 a.m. on a Sunday morning and I needed help now! I was worried everyone would be at church, and they would have trouble getting the doctors to the hospital in time. I truly believed I would not make it through the day.

The nurse's aide came strolling in. "Good morning," she said with a big smile.

The minute she looked at me and saw my belly she went running from the room. Within a matter of minutes I was floating in and out of consciousness. I don't remember seeing the doctor come in to examine me, and I am sure they had me sedated, because I don't remember being in much pain either.

I do remember my family members coming in and out to see me. Larry says he was amazed at how quickly all twelve of my siblings and their spouses got there. I remember at one point they all stood around my bed and sang praise songs. Music is a major part of our family and who I am, so it was very soothing and comforting to me. As my family sang, the music sounded like that of a room full of angels, and I wanted them to go on singing forever. I remember occasionally seeing tears, and I knew nurses were coming and going from my room in a flurry, although I don't remember actually seeing them. I vaguely remember my sister Mary standing at my bedside, stroking my head ever so gently.

The decision was made to transfer me to the I.U. Medical Center in Indianapolis, Indiana. Later, my family told me that the doctors did not have much hope for my survival, and they were very cautious not to get the family's hopes up either. I am sure those doctors were praying that I would live to make it to the I.U. Medical Center, so I would not officially die on their watch. They were more than just my doctors; they were and are my friends.

Dr. Mary McCullough has been my family doctor for over twenty years. She has stood with me and been my greatest advocate through all that I have endured. To say she's been supportive is an understatement. She is an excellent doctor and a wonderful friend, and I dread the day she retires.

I don't recall the ambulance ride to Indianapolis, but shortly after my arrival at the I.U. Medical Center ER, I do remember being whisked to a small holding room. My medications must have been wearing off because the pain was getting more and more intense, and I remember clearly that Larry and Megan were at my side. Sam arrived a few minutes later, and I didn't get to see him. In a matter of just a few minutes, the surgeon on call, Dr. Christopher Touloukian, and a nurse came rushing in.

The surgeon told Larry and Megan that he did not have time to do any X-rays or lab work. He needed to find out what he was up against before he operated. He pulled out what looked like a needle nose pliers from his pocket and, without warning, began to pull out the staples from my gaping wound.

"Hold on! What are you doing?" As he yanked out each staple, I screamed and cried from the excruciating pain. Nasty, gooey fluid oozed from my abdomen as he ripped and pulled to open the wound. The smell was nauseating and filled the room. Again without notice, he reached his entire hand into my abdomen to feel for the bowel. All the while, I wailed from the intense pain. It was more than I could endure! I wanted to die!

"Skin for skin!" Satan replied. *"A man will give all he has for his own life. But stretch out your hand and strike his flesh and bones, and he will surely curse you to your face."*

The LORD said to Satan, "Very well, then, he is in your hands; but you must spare his life" (Job 2:4-6).

Job would have the fight of his life! Satan afflicted Job with sores from the soles of his feet to the top of his head, and Job used a piece of broken pottery to scrape the sores as he sat in the ashes. There was no one to encourage Job.

Even Job's wife said, *"Are you still holding on to your integrity? Curse God and die!"*

And he replied, *"You are talking like a foolish woman. Shall we accept good from God, and not trouble? In all this, Job did not sin in what he said" (Job 2:9-10).*

Still, Job was faithful.

Chapter 5

I'm Back (January 8, 2006, I.U. Medical Center)

As may be recalled, in chapter one of this book, I shared a very detailed description of the amazing glimpse of heaven that God gave me. It was here, in the midst of the excruciating pain I was having from the surgeon pulling out staples and ripping my wound open, that I was blessed with that vision.

Then I saw myself standing in a place of brilliant light. It was the brightest pure white light I ever imagined. There was no floor and no ceiling. I was just suspended in midair! I stood in awe as I squinted and took in all the brilliant light.

I listened intently. I heard beautiful music and singing. Then I heard a voice, a male voice. I knew instantly it was Jesus.

"Today, you are coming home."

I was paralyzed with wonder and amazement! What a gift to be given – a glimpse of heaven. I will never again fear death as I look forward to heaven and all that awaits me there. I am excited that I have the promise of eternal life with Christ. Thank You, Jesus, for allowing me this very small glimpse of heaven and for this brief moment in time of the complete absence of pain and sorrow!

God poured out His incredible mercy upon me, and I will never forget those brief and precious moments. The experience has changed my life completely.

Then, just as quickly as the pain left, it was back with a vengeance! I was back in that little holding room screaming out in pain. How did this happen? I heard Dr. Touloukian tell his nurse to put me out. Those were the last words I heard. Then, Larry said I was taken straight to the operating room for emergency surgery. Finally, Dr. Touloukian came to the surgical waiting room to meet with my family and friends. There were over sixty people (family and friends from work and church) in the surgery waiting room who prayed and waited to hear the news. An additional thirty or more friends from church gathered in the hospital cafeteria because there was no more room in the surgical waiting room. Never has the love of family and friends been as evident and important as it was at that time.

The power of prayer, the power of God's Word, the omnipotent power of the Almighty and the Great I Am are indisputable. He is the Alpha and Omega, and yet, this Awesome God hears and listens to us, a lowly people whom He alone has made worthy. It is so hard to fathom why He loves us so. Praise the Lord, for He alone is Worthy of all Praise and Honor!

When Dr. Touloukian stepped into the waiting room, he asked for the Thomas family. A hush came over the room as everyone in that room turned their eyes toward him. The surgeon had no idea which people were actually my husband and children. He was amazed at the huge support system I had, and continue to have. He began to tell the news as he wiped his brow. "She made it through the surgery." Joy and praise erupted. Then everyone quickly settled down as the surgeon continued. "However, she may not make it through the night. It will certainly be touch and go, and if she does survive, she will be far from out of the woods. She will probably never eat again, and she has major complications due to the infection that has already ravaged her body. Many of her organs are severely compromised. I removed most of her intestines, but she still has about two feet of large intestines and about five and a half feet of small bowel. Also, I had to put in a colostomy."

I was taken to intensive care immediately following the surgery, where I stayed for three days. I remember waking up in the ICU a couple of days after the surgery. I wasn't quite sure where I was. I was in quite a bit of pain, and I wanted my glasses. I immediately moved my hand across my stomach. Yes, there was definitely something there. Even under all the covers and bandages, I could feel something was there. I have heard that when a patient is unconscious, or in a coma, the patient can still hear people talking and I believe that is true. I did not "remember" hearing anyone talking while I was unconscious, but I must have heard my family talking about my having a colostomy because I immediately felt for my colostomy when I woke up. I believe God allowed me to know in advance that I had the colostomy, and He allowed me the time to prepare for it even before I was conscious and verbally informed of it.

My brother Brian and sister-in-law Patti were both standing at my bedside.

"Where are my glasses?" The next question was, "Do I have a colostomy?"

Patti bent down close to me and put her hands on my face.

"You'll have to ask the surgeon about that, sweetie."

I knew then it was true. I did have a colostomy. I was not angry about the colostomy, and as soon as I was sure I had it, I was off on another thought.

However, I was really disappointed that I was still here. I couldn't imagine what had happened. I was privy to this incredible vision: a glimpse of heaven, and I really looked forward to "going home." Heaven is real and it's beyond our human comprehension! I was tired of fighting, tired of hurting, and tired of all the poking, prodding, and torturous tests. Hadn't I been through enough? What happened? Why was I still here?

Although I did not know the number of prayer warriors who were camped out all over the hospital praying and pleading for my life to be spared, I did know that my very large family and friends set into motion a network of thousands of people all over the United States who were praying for me and my family. I believe that God sometimes gives us the deepest desires of our hearts even when He knows that is not what is best for us. God heard all the heartfelt and humble moaning and groaning of His people. They were crying out for my life to be spared and God honored their prayers.

"What were they thinking?" I thought.

I looked around that ICU room for a moment and saw all kinds of monitors and machines. Each one played a vital role in my survival. I had a host of tubes coming from my body. One IV pole held at least five different bags of medications. It was frightening to think that all of this equipment was keeping my body alive. I also remember the all too familiar NG (nasal gastric tube) that came from my nose. It's a tube that was inserted up through my nose, down through my stomach and into my small bowel to suction out stomach and bowel content until my bowel "woke up" and emptied the contents on its own. It was extremely painful to have put in, and every time I moved my head the tube would move, too. It made me feel like I was constantly gagging.

"What kind of life will I have now and was I going to be a vegetable? Would I be forever dependent on machines? Were these artificial appendages, such as the colostomy, permanent, and was this how I was destined to live out the rest of my days? Would I end up in a nursing home? How could my family afford all of this? I would have been so much better off if I had died as I believed I would."

I was still stunned and tried to cope with the fact that I hadn't died. I was so certain that I was going to be in heaven with Jesus. I remember thinking, "Be careful what you pray for. You just might get it!" I contemplated my dilemma.

"Lord, please show me why I'm still here. Help me understand Your plan for my life. How can I serve You when I am such a physical mess?"

I wondered how I could be a light in the darkness if I couldn't even get out of bed. No answer came, but God did bring peace to my troubled soul. I was to remain on this earth, and I was to continue to be a witness in all I endure and become. That seemed to be a pretty tall order in my present state, but I knew in my spirit that I would not remain in that condition. God would deliver me. I did my best to trust Him in all of it, and I tried to praise Him in all circumstances, even in the most difficult of adversities. Many times my faith was shaken, but not destroyed. God honored my prayers and the prayers of His people, and He gave me the strength to remain faithful; for that I have continued to praise Him.

It was so good to see all of my family! Two at a time they came in with the biggest smiles, hugs and kisses. Wow, I have the best family! When I saw Larry and the children I was so overwhelmed I could barely talk. I was so happy to have more time with them. I was still needed, and God had a purpose for me being here. He wasn't finished with me, and I knew He would show me in time. That was a wonderful feeling.

Chapter 6

This is Not Going to be Fun!
(January 2006, I.U. Medical Center)

As the days progressed, I slowly began to improve, and after a few days I was moved to another floor. I was used to the constant attention in the Intensive Care Unit, and it would be much different on the surgical floor. The day I was moved from ICU one of the wound care nurses came to see me. Some of my family was there visiting with me in my room.

She came to show me and a family member how to care for my colostomy and how to change the dressing on my surgical wound. She also mentioned that she would be hooking up a Wound Vac machine. I had no idea what I was in for. I was on some very heavy pain medications and could barely comprehend what she was saying.

The wound nurse looked around the room at all my visitors and asked, "Who here is family and which one is here to learn how to care for her colostomy?" I could see sheer panic on their faces. Everyone took a step back. No one expected that! I didn't know what to say, and there was absolute silence for a few seconds.

Finally, my husband said, "I'm not home every day. I'll learn so I can do it when I'm home, but someone else will have to do it when I'm gone."

My children were both in college and they would not be home to help me.

My sister Anna looked around the room for a moment and said, "I'm not good at this kind of thing, but I'll try. I just don't want to be the only one to learn it."

I felt so bad for my family. I knew they were terrified, and scared to death to even touch me. I was scared to touch myself, and I had no idea just how big and nasty my wound was. In fact, I was in for a very rude awakening! The nurse got right up in my face. She said, "This is not going to be fun, but we'll get through it, and it is going to be okay."

I knew then that I was in for some real pain. She began to gently pull back the bandages. It was very uncomfortable. The more layers she peeled back, the more pain. As she got closer to the wound, the pain became unbearable! I winced and tried to hold back the tears, but I could not take the pain. Finally, the nurse stopped and got another nurse to come in and give me some additional pain medication.

The wound nurse said, "We'll just wait a minute to let the pain medications start working." I was extremely thankful for her compassion!

Then the nurse began telling us all about her job and her hobbies. As she spoke she kept working, and tried to keep me engaged in the conversation as much as possible. Little by little, I could see the beginning of a huge cavern! There were no stitches! I mean NO stitches at all! No wonder I was in so much pain. I had an open wound that was about nine inches long and about four inches deep in places! My face went completely pale and very hot. I started to shake uncontrollably, and I literally thought I would vomit. Unfortunately, my family felt the same. The nurse grabbed the emesis basin.

The horror on their faces said it all. Removing the bandages was very painful, but seeing the pain and anguish on the faces of my family was really hard to swallow. I remember thinking the wound looked as if it was cut with a chainsaw, and with all the blood and raw, exposed tissue, it was like something seen in a horror film. The nurse leaned over me and secured my left arm as she prepared to clean inside the wound.

"Oh, please God, help me! I can't take this!"

I held on for dear life. I thought nothing could be worse than that pain, but I was wrong! The nurse used sterile gauze and saline to clean inside the wound. When she finished cleaning it, she packed the entire wound with what looked like big black sponges. She could not hold me down any longer. I moaned and groaned and wiggled all over the place. The sponge material was semi-pliable, but still fairly stiff. It felt as if she was shoving sand paper in my wound. Over and over, large chunks of foam were thrust deep inside my wound, and I silently prayed to die. The pain medication I was given a few minutes earlier had completely worn off. When the nurse finally finished packing the wound, I was exhausted and dripping with sweat, but she wasn't quite finished yet.

"Oh, that I might have my request that God would grant what I hope for, that God would be willing to crush me, to let loose his hand and cut me off! Then I would still have this consolation – my joy in unrelenting pain – that I had not denied the words of the Holy One" (Job 6:8-10).

"Please, stop! I can't take this!" I was desperate for it to be over.

"Yes, you can," the nurse said in a very soft voice, and she moved on to the colostomy.

Her eyes rarely left mine, and I was more than relieved to find out that changing the colostomy appliances was not quite as painful. Pulling the tape and old appliance off was the worst part, but even then, it was tolerable. When she removed the plastic bag that covered my colostomy, I was aghast to see how my intestines were coming out from inside of me! They were attached to the surface of my abdomen.

"This lovely opening is called the stoma," the nurse said. It seemed that everyone in the room gasped. I did. Again, I watched the faces of my family. They could not stand to watch, and yet they were so curious that they had to watch. She showed Anna how to measure, cut, and apply the flange, the appliance that would adhere to my abdomen, and how to attach the bag. My system was a little more of a challenge than the average colostomy patient to manage, because my stoma was less than two inches from the left side of my open surgical wound. There wasn't much flat skin left to attach the colostomy appliances. I had a lot of skin folds from the surgery, so the nurse was having significant trouble getting the appliance to seal without any leaks. After twenty minutes or so, success! Everyone let out a big sigh of relief.

"Thank goodness, we're done," I thought and I fell back onto my pillow. I was completely spent. I pushed on my pain pump button frantically, but it just couldn't deliver fast enough.

"We're almost done, Debbie," the wound nurse looked so pleased.

"Almost, what do you mean, almost?"

"The worst part is over and from here on out it's just a matter of cleaning and bandaging the fistula, and adding the Wound Vac. The Wound Vac will heal your wound in half the time! This will be a piece of cake."

She really felt awful about the pain I endured, but it was necessary. Now she was ready to tackle the abdominal fistula. Fistulas are tracks or tunnels that form because there is an area, pocket, or abscess in the body that is under pressure, and that pressure needs to be relieved. Shortly after my surgery, my body formed two fistulas.

When my colostomy was fashioned, Dr. Touloukian cut the bowel in two places. I had a section of bowel attached to the base of my stomach and another section attached to my rectum. All the intestines in between were removed. They were damaged beyond repair, and the surgeon removed all but seven and a half feet of bowel.

The section of small bowel that is attached to my stomach, which is about five and a half feet long, was pulled up and attached to the surface of my abdomen to create my new colostomy opening or stoma. The contents from my stomach pass through this small section of bowel to the stoma protruding at the surface of my abdomen. The contents are then eliminated into a plastic bag.

The other section of bowel, eighteen inches of colon that is attached to my rectum, was tied off at the opposite end and no longer functions. I refer to it as a "tail" section, because it is a fairly long section of colon that is just floating around in my abdomen. It really serves no purpose at this point, but nonetheless, it is still there.

As I said earlier, I had two fistulas. The abdominal fistula actually connected the two sections of surgically separated bowel together at the center of each bowel section, creating the appearance of the letter "H." The fistula tunneled to the surface of my abdomen where it created a hole, about the size of a dime, just a couple of inches below my surgical wound. This opening stayed red and irritated all the time. Sometimes it bled, but mostly it drained thick brownish or green infection, and it smelled as terrible as it looked. Occasionally, after several rounds of antibiotics, the hole formed a thin layer of skin over it. I used to think that meant it was healed. However, as the pressure built up just below the skin's surface, it eventually erupted and spewed everywhere. That was not a pretty sight! The abdominal fistula drained for years. I had so many infections from the slow bowel leaks that it was almost four and a half years, and several surgeries later, before the abdominal fistula finally closed up for good.

The second fistula is located near my tailbone. It starts in the lower "tail" section of my bowel and has tunneled through the abdominal tissue alongside my tailbone. The fistula and the tissues around the tailbone become inflamed at times, and trigger tremendous tailbone and low back pain. Because of the fistula's substantial size, and the fact that it has been there for almost six years now, the surgeon believes it will never close. The wound nurse finished the cleanup and dressing of the abdominal fistula, and it was relatively painless. By this time, I felt very relieved that we were finally done, and I was ready to rest.

Then the nurse almost whispered that she still needed to apply the Wound Vac. She had already packed my wound, and now she covered the entire wound and surrounding area with a plastic wrapping that resembled large sheets of clear packing tape. It took about twenty minutes to apply the tape. Finally, a small circular suction device was placed directly over the center of the wound, and then the nurse turned on the machine.

The machine began to suction air out of the wound, and the sponges began to shrink. It reminded me of the Space Bags seen on TV, as it shriveled up tight against my skin. Initially, the "shrinking" sensation was uncomfortable. However, as it continued to shrink and shrivel it actually helped to pull the wound together, and it gave me a sense of support! It was the weirdest process I'd ever seen, and when it was completely suctioned down I felt like I could move without fear of ripping the wound open. I was thankful for that!

There was one aspect of the Wound Vac that really bothered me. I am allergic to plastic tape, and it causes my skin to break down. I knew the plastic covering the nurse was using with the Wound Vac would have the same effect, but they could not use any other type of tape. I had a sick feeling in the pit of my stomach that it was going to be arduous and agonizing to remove the plastic every three days! I knew my skin would be a real mess!

At last we were finished. I survived the first round of bandage changes. All the trash was cleaned up, and the nurse asked everyone to leave the room so I could rest. She ordered another dose of pain medication for me and stayed with me for a few minutes while the medication took effect. She held my hand and rubbed it gently. She told me what a good job I did coping with all she did, but I didn't think I'd done quite so well. She just held my hand while she spoke ever so gently to me, and before I knew it I was fast asleep.

Chapter 7

I Didn't Sign Up for This
(January 2006, I.U. Medical Center)

Every three days the wound nurses came and changed the bandage and appliances. Each time, family members would have to watch so they could help me at home. They struggled not to make faces of disgust, but their eyes could not lie. Just seeing that big, I mean BIG, open wound was bad enough, let alone having to mess with my colostomy.

I was right; removing all the plastic tape was torture! My skin broke down from the tape being pulled off and reapplied. I had big patches of soupy sores, so the nurses dabbed milk of magnesia over the sores with cotton balls so the sores would dry. The milk of magnesia formed an artificial layer that was supposed to protect the sores from the next taping. It did seem to help a little, but ripping off the plastic tape time and time again really took its toll on my skin. The nurse tried pulling very slowly and she tried ripping quickly. Slow and steady was the better method, and was the easiest on the raw patches of skin.

I was constantly aggravated by the NG tube in my nose. My nose was so raw from the tube rubbing against it that it bled almost everyday. I could not wait to get that tube taken out, but the surgeon was not about to remove it until he was sure everything was working as it should. I needed to be patient, no matter how uncomfortable it was.

Doctors and nurses don't like to sedate patients when they put NG tubes in because they claim it only takes about ten minutes to put it in. My experience has been that the whole ordeal takes at least half an hour, and it feels more like an hour of pure torture! So many times I wanted to take that tube and shove it up the nose of a nurse who said, "It's not that big of a deal!" I know that doesn't sound very Christian-like, but that is exactly how I felt at the time. I can remember at least two or three times when a nurse tried to ram an NG tube up my nose, and by the time she was finished, I was drenched in blood.

I certainly did not want the tube to come out early, only to find out that they would have to put it back in. So I prayed that God would help me to cope with the pain and irritation of the tube, and visitors would not be too uncomfortable when they'd see the nasty drainage in the tube.

Two years ago I saw an ENT (ear, nose and throat specialist). I told the doctor that I was having frequent nosebleeds. I also told him about all the NG tubes I had had over the years and the difficulties the nurses had getting the tubes in.

The doctor explained that much of the cartilage between the left and right sides of my nose was missing, and what was left was scarred and damaged. He said I have an irregular shaped hole in the middle of the cartilage. Ironically, the diameter of the hole is about the size of a nasal gastric tube. He also said the damage is permanent and will likely continue to cause nosebleeds. The ENT was right; I have had numerous nosebleeds and some were very serious.

In February of 2011 while I was being discharged from a stay at Decatur County Memorial Hospital, my nose started bleeding. The nurses did not feel the nosebleed was anything significant, so they let me go home. At home I developed a migraine headache, and my nose continued bleeding non-stop for over twelve hours. I went to the ER where the doctor packed my nose and sent me home. A few hours later I passed out in my bathroom, and I ended up being admitted to the hospital. My blood pressure was almost non-existent, and I was given two pints of blood.

I absolutely refuse to have another NG tube put in without some kind of sedation! Yes, it takes a few minutes longer, but EVERYONE comes out of it much happier! Patients have rights and NO ONE should have to endure the agony of having an NG tube put in without sedation. When Dr. Alunday put in my last NG tube, he sedated me as requested, and I really appreciated that! Thankfully, other NG tubes were put in while I was in surgery, and I was totally unaware of it.

I began to have more and more trouble sleeping, so Dr. Touloukian ordered sleep medication for me in the hospital. It made me have horrible dreams, and I was trying to get out of bed in the middle of the night without knowing it. That didn't go over well with the nurses. I seem to have adverse reactions to some medications, and this sleep medication was no exception.

One night I tried to take all the bedding off my bed. I woke up with my head at the foot of my bed, my gown all up around my neck, and the sheets snarled around my feet. A couple of nurses tried to get me turned around. I was in so much pain, and I was tangled in my IV tubing, and I pulled on my Wound Vac so hard that I almost broke the seal on it.

The nurses were determined to make sure I didn't do that again. They sat me in a chair and straightened up the linens on my bed. Then they helped me back into bed and tied my hands to the bed rails! I fought them the entire time! They called for a third nurse, and she put medication in my IV line.

It wasn't my fault! It wasn't as if I did this on purpose. I begged them to let me go, and I promised not to get out of bed or move around if they would just untie me, but they would not. I felt like I'd done something horrible, and I was being punished for it. It seemed so cruel. After a couple of minutes of fighting it seemed my whole body went limp. I don't know what kind of medication the nurse gave me, but I was definitely not going to be getting out of bed, so why tie me down? Before I knew it, I was out.

In the morning, I begged to be untied. My roommate put the call light on for me, but it seemed like forever before they finally came and untied me. I was so happy to have my hands free! It felt absolutely horrible being held down against my will, and it was very scary. I know it was for my own good, but at the time, I did not believe it for one moment!

I was afraid some of my family might not want to visit because of how awful I looked, or for fear that they might be roped into helping with my wound or colostomy care. They did not sign up for all this, and it wasn't their responsibility! Praise God, they committed to help, despite how difficult it was for them. When I prayed, I thanked God continually for my family. They kept coming back and loving me more each day. I certainly did not deserve all they did for me, but I was so thankful for them!

Although I was determined to do whatever it would take to get well, I did not have the slightest idea of how I could care for myself at home. I had to rely on my family. I was so apologetic about it, but I didn't know what else to do. The wound nurse was having tremendous difficulty getting the colostomy and the Wound Vac to seal, and she was very frustrated by the skin irritations and sores caused from plastic tape.

I thought, "She's the professional, and if she's having problems, how are we supposed to manage all this at home?" I was overwhelmed, to say the least.

Poor Anna was overwhelmed, too. She'd put on her best face in front of me, but I know she wanted to run like fire! I did, too, but I wanted to go home even more. To accomplish my goal, I would have to learn how to do some of the care myself, especially the colostomy care! I also needed to change my attitude about my colostomy.

I needed to keep my focus on Christ, as He would be my strength. I really believed that I would get well because God did such wonderful healing in me already. However, my attitude was preventing me from further recovery, and I couldn't understand why I was feeling so disturbed about everything. Besides the roller coaster of emotions, I had raging hot flashes, and lots of cramping in my shins.

I wondered if my hormones were out of balance. I asked the surgeon if he ordered any hormone testing and he said, "Yes." He told me that my hormone level was so low it didn't even register, but I could not have any hormone replacement therapy because I was such a high risk for blood clots. The absence of hormones explained a lot about how I was feeling!

I knew a positive attitude would impact how well I felt and healed, but I wasn't quite sure how I could be so positive when I didn't have any hormones! I had to constantly remind myself that God was in control, and I begged God to get me through. At the time, I didn't realize the value of my prayer time with Jesus. The actual act of prayer became a means of refocusing. I needed Him to help me keep my mind focused and "stayed on Him."

God knew just what I needed, and He provided relief that was much better than hormone therapy! I believe that's what helped me not to be bitter about my circumstances. How could I be focused on God, recognize all that He had done for me, experience so many blessings, and be bitter? It wasn't possible. When my mind was filled with Jesus, there was no room for bitterness! I couldn't be mad at God when I was focused on Him.

I tried to be so brave, but there were times when I took my eyes off God and I complained about the strife in my life or wallowed in self-pity. I found myself questioning God, and my mind filled with negatives. I knew I could not stay in that place, because it would lead to a bad attitude, pride, arrogance, and bitterness. I had to keep redirecting my focus, and when I'd get on a tangent, I reverted to God! Occasionally, when everyone went home, I curled up into a little ball and just cried. Crying never made it easier, but I couldn't control my emotions anymore. I know my lack of hormones played a role in my instability; however, I can't blame it all on that. God had not allowed Satan to take my life, so Satan worked another angle – Satan wanted my mind. I knew a war waged against my body, but now there was a fight for my mind, too. Never had I coveted prayers as I did then, and I never appreciated the few Scriptures I'd memorized more! I clung to God's Word and promises. At times, it seemed God literally lifted me up off my bed and pulled me aside. He looked deep into my eyes and said, "I am with you and I am enough."

He was. I often thought of the Scripture, *You* (God) *will keep in perfect peace him* (me) *whose mind is steadfast because he* (I) *trusts in you* (God). *Trust in the LORD forever, for the LORD, the LORD, is the Rock eternal (Isaiah 26:3-4).*

Thank You, Lord, for Your Word! You are my ROCK!

Job struggled with his emotions, too, and he was miserable. Not only had he lost all his possessions, he lost his family! He was covered in oozing sores, sitting in ashes, and praying for relief. I couldn't begin to imagine his pain. He didn't have the luxury of a nice clean hospital, doctors and nurses to care for him, or pain medication to ease his suffering.

How did Job remain blameless when he was so beaten down physically and emotionally?

When Job's three friends, Eliphaz the Temanite, Bildad the Shuhite, and Zophar the Naamathite, heard about all the troubles that had come upon him, they set out from their homes and met together by agreement to go and sympathize with him and comfort him. When they saw him from a distance they could hardly recognize him; they began to weep aloud, and they tore their robes and sprinkled dust on their heads. Then they sat on the ground with him for seven days and seven nights. No one said a word to him, because they saw how great his suffering was (Job 2:11-13).

"My face is red with weeping, deep shadows ring my eyes; yet my hands have been free of violence and my prayer is pure" (Job 16:16-17).

When Job lost his focus on God, he was consumed with how atrocious he felt, and his immeasurable loss. He could not see good in any of it, and Job felt so dreadful that he wanted to die! He was really angry at his friends for their accusations, and was becoming bitter. Job needed to get his focus back on God! He needed to remember how God had always provided for him. Job recalled times when his life was good, and he wanted for nothing, and he welcomed those moments of refreshment. He remembered his family and how he loved celebrating with them. He also remembered how he prospered and how he was able to help those less fortunate. Job's ability to remember and recall those times was a blessing in itself.

If nothing else, Job remembered experiences when he knew God walked with him, provided for him, and provided joy for him. I believe that is what sustained Job time and time again. When Job focused on God, he remained blameless.

One way Job remained focused on God was by continuously talking to Him. Notice how Job talked about his problems and how he questioned God, but then he'd turn right around and praise God. He knew and trusted in God's faithfulness! Job kept his mind "stayed on God." In all his conversation, Job talked to God, NOT AT God!

Chapter 8

A Really Bad Attitude
(Mid January 2006, I.U. Medical Center)

Boy, did I ever have an attitude about my colostomy! I didn't complain to everyone, but I did complain to God. I told God all the time how much I was struggling with the colostomy, and I told God how mad I was when I ended up literally drenched in poop! Oh, yes, God knew just exactly how I felt! I mostly prayed that I would be able to have the menace reversed!

Dr. Touloukian told me there might be a possibility one day of having my colostomy reversed, and I counted on it. In fact, I basically waged war against my colostomy! That was not good! I had a terrible attitude and I knew it, but what I didn't realize was that God would change that!

It was especially sickening to awake to stool leaking down my side and leg. It was all over my bedding, too, and I'd have to lie in it until the nurse could get me cleaned up. I know it washes off, but it made me feel so dirty and nasty!

The colostomy bag itself was clear because the nurses needed to see what kind of output I produced. Seeing the stool in the bag lying on my abdomen made me want to throw up. It felt dirty against my skin even when the contents were completely contained in the bag and only the plastic actually touched my skin.

The smell was awful, too! My stomach and bowel made all kinds of noises, and I had a lot of gas. It was difficult for my very short gut to manage the methane gas produced. Yes, I said "methane gas." The wound nurse explained that digested food produces methane gas. That's where the old jokes about bad gas and matches came from. For most people gas is eliminated through the rectum. The intense odor of the methane gas is diffused and loses its pungent stench as it continues down the long, large intestines and completes the digestion process. The gas stinks, but by the time it's finally eliminated out the rectum, it no longer has the distinct smell of methane gas.

In colostomy patients, the methane gas is released in its typically pungent state into the colostomy bag. It definitely has a very distinct smell, and I feel I can smell that odor all the time, even when others around me say they can't. I'm not sure if they are being completely truthful with me or not, but I sure hope they are.

God taught me about humility. I began trying very hard to accept the colostomy as a part of my body; after all, it was a vital part that allowed me to process food and to LIVE. Still, I struggled, and it was a day to day process.

My colostomy issues weighed heavily on my heart. Everyday I prayed for forgiveness for my attitude and that God would help me to deal with the trouble I had with the colostomy. I also prayed that I could learn to laugh instead of cry when accidents occurred. In time, I found myself offering prayers of gratitude. I thanked God that He gave me Larry and Anna, and that they were willing to help me care for my wound and colostomy. I wanted others to see that I was able to manage my colostomy with God's help, and that they could, too! I asked God for JOY in the midst of it all! Slowly, but surely, God changed my heart and mind.

Job endured so much, and he began to really believe that he might have offended God, and this was his punishment. *"… Why have you made me your target? Have I become a burden to you? Why do you not pardon my offenses and forgive my sins? For I will soon lie down in the dust; you will search for me, but I will be no more" (Job 7:20-21).*

Job was human and he was broken. He had no idea of God's plan, so Job continued to question why he endured so many horrible problems. God loved Job and what God had waiting for Job would be far better than Job could ever dream of having. Were Job's problems a result of his lack of faith, or was he plagued with problems because his faith was deemed worthy of testing? It must have seemed that God didn't care about his suffering because Job could find no comfort. Did God even care if Job was happy or not? Job was absolutely miserable!

I believe God wanted to shower Job with sweet relief, but He wanted Satan to see that Job was faithful even when he had nothing to gain from it. God cared more about Job being a man of Godly character, and He wanted Job to achieve real joy instead of momentary happiness. Job's faithfulness in all of his tribulations would eventually bring him the ultimate joy he longed for.

Remember, Satan asked Jesus to let him test His servant, Job. For Job, I would say he was deemed worthy of testing. If so, his problems came as a means of testing, and he would come out of it with an even greater understanding of faith and true joy. That's exactly what happened!

I wondered if God was more interested in my character, too. Was He just going to let me suffer to prove a point or for me to learn a lesson? Maybe so; I had no idea of God's plan for me either. Were all my problems a result of my lack of faith or because my faith was deemed worthy of testing? It would be prideful of me to think I was worthy of testing. I don't know if I would ever reach the level of faith that Job had in the midst of his most challenging problems, but I did desire to honor God in all my circumstances; good and bad, and to be found blameless before Him.

I have grown so much in my faith and relationship with Jesus. My character has become more Christ-like; still I am not sinless. Neither was Job. What level of character constitutes a level of worthiness for testing? Only God knows that. If my problems are a result of a lack of faith, my faith will increase, thus causing my character to be more Christ-like and proving me to be more worthy of testing and true joy. Still, I question if it really matters if the result is that we come to be more Christ-like and know true joy? It's as confusing as the age old saying; "Which came first, the chicken or the egg?" Is there a right or wrong answer? I think at some point in our walk with Christ, if we are truly committed to growing in our relationship with Him, we will find we lack faith, and at another point we will be worthy of testing.

Chapter 9

Laughter Really is the Best Medicine
(Mid January 2006, I.U. Medical Center)

God answered so many of my prayers, and He gave me Joy and laughter, especially when I least expected it! One day my wound nurse told my roommate and me about a colostomy patient who was having problems with gas. The nurse was very animated when she talked, so I knew we were in for a real treat. She made the most disgusting faces, and she waved her arms all over the place. She lowered her voice and almost whispered; then she'd speak louder, and vividly described the event.

She had a colostomy patient who was in his 80's when he got his colostomy. She warned him not to eat gassy foods, because the gas in a colostomy bag is actually methane gas! The nurse also wanted him to understand how serious it could be if he didn't watch what he ate! She pointed her finger at me as she drove home her point. Anyway, she said it is possible to have so much gas that it will completely fill the bag, and the bag can literally blow off. Well, this guy didn't believe her and didn't care anyway. He was old, and nobody would tell him what he could or couldn't eat! Well, he ate something one night that made him extremely gassy. Every few minutes he "burped" his bag; letting off some of the gas so it wouldn't fill up and blow off. His roommate, who was much younger, was about to gag from the smell!

As the nurse told the story, I could just imagine a green haze of gas floating over his bed and his poor roommate crouched under his covers, trying to keep from breathing the fumes. The old man "burped" his bag all evening and, by bedtime, he figured the gas was pretty much under control. His nurse was in and out and couldn't help but notice the horrendous smell. She offered several times to have his doctor order medication to help relieve the gas, but the old man refused. I'll bet that nurse was trying to do a favor for the roommate. If she was bothered by the smell, it must have been truly appalling for his poor roommate. She remarked that the roommate was a "real saint," because he never once complained to the old man about the smell. Finally, the old man drifted off to sleep.

The wound nurse had a big smile sweep across her face and started to laugh so hard she could barely finish the story. My roommate and I kept telling her to settle down and tell us what happened. By this time we were all laughing uncontrollably because we knew what was coming. Well, you guessed it – the bag filled completely with gas and all of a sudden it exploded – literally exploded! That bag was full of gas and poop! The nurse said it sounded like a bomb when it blew off! Not only did the bag blow off and land on the floor across the room, but poop flew everywhere. Disgusting! She said there was poop on the window blinds, in the air vents, and even in the roommate's hair! Yuck!!! Nurses ran from every direction to see what happened. She said the old man was shocked, and he never moved. He just lay there with his hands raised up off his bed, which was also covered in poop, and he simply looked at everyone with the most pitiful countenance as if he was going to cry.

As the nurse told the story, we all continued laughing so hard we could barely breathe. She went on to say that she was called to put a new colostomy appliance on the old man. When she walked into that room; she walked right back out to get a mask, a gown, booties and two sets of gloves. The stink nearly knocked her over. She gave both men a complete bath and changed all the linens before she could even think about working on the old man's colostomy. She cleaned up the roommate first because she thought he deserved it since he suffered so much. When she started to bathe the old man she kept a towel draped over his stoma to prevent being drenched if it blew again. She waved her hands in an up and down motion and said the towel kept "poofing" up and down as it lay over his stoma, and he continued to have horrible gas! Never, in all her years of nursing, had she seen anything like that!

Oh, my, we were laughing so loudly we just knew we would get into big trouble for disturbing the other patients! The nurse said the poor janitor was in the old man's room for over three hours cleaning poop off the walls and out of all the little crevices in the room. By the time the nurse finished her story and my roommate and I finally got control of ourselves, our stomachs were killing us! I requested additional pain medicine because I was hurting so badly.

My roommate threatened me with my life if I were ever to do that to her. We just started right back up laughing. In the middle of the night we both found ourselves laughing again! Gosh, we laughed for days over that story. It was the very best medicine either of us could have ever been prescribed! I thanked the Lord over and over again for His gracious gift of laughter, and I was also very careful in selecting the vegetables I had with my meals.

There is a tremendous release of stress when one laughs. Laughter breaks down walls and stops me in my tracks. It makes me take notice of what I am allowing to drive my emotions. It permits me to be less serious. It's okay for me to lighten up and laugh, especially at myself.

Chapter 10

A Lesson in Humility
(Mid January 2006, I.U. Medical Center)

Believe it or not, I used to be a very shy person. I was very modest, and I was quiet, so it was extremely difficult for me to be constantly exposed. The residents and nurses tried their best to keep me covered while they examined me, but it certainly did not meet my standards. Because the hospital is a teaching hospital, there were never less than five or six residents in my room "checking me over" at the same time. Everyone needed to see what was going on. I know the doctors and nurses have seen it all before, but at times, I felt like a sideshow. I needed their help, yet I hated that I had so little privacy. I was at their mercy, and I prayed for God to help me get past the awkward feelings and anxiety of exposure.

"I have become a laughingstock to my friends, though I called upon God and He answered – a mere laughingstock, though righteous and blameless!" (Job 12:4).

Truthfully, the residents had no idea how sensitive I was. I wasn't really mad at them; I was more embarrassed than anything. I understood that was the process to get the care I needed, and God taught me a lot about humility. As I learned to move past the issue of embarrassment, I began to focus on another issue that troubled me; I wanted so badly to be used by God. I did not want to be so out of touch, physically or emotionally, with the outside world that it would be very difficult for me to be used for the glory of God. God did so many miracles in my life, and I wanted to share that with everyone. How could I spread the Good News when I was flat on my back in a hospital bed?

I saw myself as broken – a cracked pot. Similar to a cracked pot, I was loaded with imperfections and faults. I felt my ability to share Christ with others was slipping right through the cracks.

Little did I know those tiny crevices in my life – the ones I thought rendered me useless, would become real blessings. My physical condition became something that opened doors for sharing intimate and life-changing conversations with a host of people. I was humbled to serve, to share the love of Jesus, and to offer hope to the hopeless.

My heart ached for my roommate because of her intense pain … and because she seldom had the luxury of family there to encourage her. I felt compelled to share, to encourage, and to offer compassion to other hurting patients, as well as my nurses and doctors. I began to understand that I still had a vital purpose for Christ, and I could be used for His glory and honor. I would be able to reach many people for Christ as a result of my adversities. I just had to find new avenues to do it, and I now refer to my struggles and adversities as "opportunities," because of what they did for me.

Alberta, a very wise and dear friend from church, is a shining example of how we can overcome our struggles. She taught me the value of adversities and how important it is to see them as opportunities, rather than problems. She's been through so much herself, and she has been a tremendous role model for me. These opportunities have caused me to be a much more humble person, and they gave me a real understanding of despair and hope. My adversities, now opportunities, have opened many doors for me to share Christ, and I am beginning to see that my journey with God is taking me in a whole new direction. God is leading me down different avenues – ones that will allow me more exposure and opportunities to share Jesus with others.

My friends from work gave me a basket full of gifts while I was in the hospital, and there was a devotional book written by Max Lucado. That book became very special to me and to my roommate. I also had a small CD player and a CD of Jim Brickman, composed of soft instrumental praise music, and I loved it. I played it all day long! The first time I played it, I kept the music turned down very low so I would not disturb my roommate. She heard "Amazing Grace" playing, and she asked me to turn it up. I found out she loved music, and we discovered all sorts of interests we had in common. From then on, our room was filled with music.

Each morning I said my prayers and then read one of Max Lucado's short devotionals. One morning when I finished, I told my roommate what the devotional offered, and we shared a little about how it applied to our own lives. The next day I did the same, and then the third day, before I even had my book out, my roommate asked if I would read the devotional to her. I did, and we had a wonderful discussion afterwards. That book provided the encouragement we both needed at just the right time.

God gave me someone very special – the gift of my roommate, and He gave me to her. The day she asked me to read my devotion aloud was the day I truly knew that God could use me in any shape or form, even as a cracked pot! She was the perfect roommate, and we spent hours sharing together. God is so good to give us exactly what we need. I really loved her, and she was such a wonderful friend to me. I was grateful she allowed me to be such a part of her life.

Except for the presence of God, there were times that we felt we were all alone. In the long, dark hours of the night, we had each other and that was it. We were there in that hospital room for an entire month. Many times it felt like we'd been there for several months, and at times it felt as if it had only been a few days. When the resident talked about transferring me to another floor, I was so sad. Being transferred to another floor was a very good sign, and it meant I was that much closer to getting to go home, but I was sad because I knew I would miss my roommate terribly.

The day came for my transfer, and I really wanted to do something special for my roommate, so I prayed about what I could do for her. After I prayed, I looked around the room to see what I possessed that might be a blessing to her, and I saw the book. Perfect! I gave her my Max Lucado devotional. She cried and so did I. I praised God for our friendship and for allowing me to find my purpose again.

Job was a man after God's own heart. Every morning he went to God in prayer and he sacrificed a burnt offering to Him. What a way to start the day! God's just waiting for me to come to Him, and when I do, He is always there to listen. He loves me so much.

... Early in the morning he would sacrifice a burnt offering

for each of them, thinking, "Perhaps my children have sinned and cursed God in their hearts." This was Job's regular custom (Job 1:5).

Job was not only concerned about his soul, but those of his children as well. When we experience the freedom of grace and salvation, we want to share it with everyone we meet. In the book of Matthew we are charged to go forth and spread the good news, preaching the gospel to the entire world. It is a privilege to be used of God and to share the gospel with others. We should be concerned about the souls of everyone.

Chapter 11

Battle Scars (Mid January 2006, I.U. Medical Center)

For the most part, my nurses were very good, and I had excellent care. Unfortunately, there always seems to be one nurse in every hospital who has lost the passion for helping people, and has forgotten the promise to be both a help and an advocate for the patient. I have many battle scars from physical wounds, but sometimes the emotional wounds leave the most painful battle scars of all.

It was in the early morning hours, but I was wide awake and wanted to sit up. I was restless and I needed my glasses because I am legally blind without them, and it's very frightening if I don't have them. Just then, a nurse came in to take my vitals. She was an older nurse, and she kind of wobbled when she walked. I'll never forget her! She chomped on her gum the way a horse chews carrots. She popped her gum, and it was loud, annoying, and rude!

I asked her to please hand me my glasses, which were about two feet away on my side table, but she didn't answer and just kept messing with the blood pressure machine. She shoved the blood pressure cuff on my arm.

"Can I please have my glasses? I can't see anything without them," I said.

"You don't need them. I'm almost done here, and you can go right back to sleep," she snapped, as she kept chomping her gum like there was no tomorrow.

I said, "I'm sorry, but I can't sleep. That's the problem, and I want my glasses."

She bellowed sternly, "I said, NO. We are short-staffed, and we can't be watching you all night. Now, just turn over and go to sleep."

"I can't roll over. Could you please help me with my pillows?"

She did not respond, and proceeded to move my side table to the foot of my bed, so there was no chance I could get to my glasses. I couldn't believe it! I had no idea why she was so cruel. As she left the room, I began crying and eventually cried myself to sleep. I was so emotional anyway, but this was just uncalled for, and no one should be treated that way. I was hurt, really hurt. It was such a simple request, and I was crushed that she withheld something so important from me.

The next morning I told the incoming nurse what had happened. The nurse handed me my glasses and moved my side table back to the head of my bed. She felt badly for what had taken place, but clearly she had no idea how much it affected me emotionally.

I could definitely tell this nurse had no intention of taking any action regarding my complaint. I didn't want last night's nurse fired. I simply wanted her to be made aware of the serious impact her actions made on me. I would have loved an apology, but that wasn't going to happen. Fortunately, I never saw the cruel nurse again, and it was as if she disappeared off the face of the earth.

From that moment on, I never took my glasses off my face while I was in that hospital. I even slept in them, and the only time I removed them was when I had a procedure that prevented me from wearing them or while I was in surgery. That nurse will never know the damage she did in that one cruel act. Even today, in the privacy of my own home, many times I still sleep with my glasses on.

"When I lie down I think 'How long before I get up?' The night drags on, and I toss till dawn" (Job 7:4). "Therefore I will not keep silent; I will speak out in the anguish of my spirit, I will complain in the bitterness of my soul ... When I think my bed will comfort me and my couch will ease my complaint, even then you frighten me with dreams and terrify me with visions" (Job 7:11; 13-14).

Many nights I went without sleep, and even today, I suffer from horrible insomnia. The nights were long and hard. My wheels spun and my heart cried out to God. I did a lot of praying in the night. Sometimes, I felt like Job in that I sensed my prayers were insignificant, and that I should not bother God with such silly needs as sleep and glasses.

Maybe this Majestic and Mighty God would not deem such requests worthy of answering. While I desperately wanted answers, I felt awkward as I continued asking God for answers. I was wrong to feel that way, because God wants to acknowledge all our concerns and prayers. We should expect that He will communicate with us. He loves us and wants us to understand how He cares about every detail in our lives.

As parents, we don't always give our children a clear cut answer to their questions, but we do listen and we do care. We refrain, at times, from giving the full answer or supplying all their needs at once.

"Why do you complain to him that he answers none of man's words? For God does speak – now one way, now another – though man may not perceive it" (Job 33:13-14).

Job's friends chastised him for expecting God to answer him. Job did not demand answers from God, but he did ask, expecting answers. Job was right and his friends were wrong, and God confirmed this when he said to Job's friends, *"I am angry with you and your two friends, because you have not spoken of me what is right, as my servant Job has" (Job 42:7).*

Job was right to keep the communication lines open between him and God, and he never shut God out. He was human and had times of frustration and self-pity, but still he did not sin against God. That communication and prayer helped him focus. Job felt the need to cry out to God, and he wanted to be heard; Job had questions, yet he knew his place. He was honest with God in sharing his anguish, but he acknowledged who God is and His authority, and he acknowledged that no wisdom surpasses that of God.

Still, God wants us to talk to Him; He wants to hear from His children. He knows we are human and will not understand all that is before us. There is comfort in relinquishing control over to a Sovereign God, knowing He will take our concerns and He will answer. We can drop our heavy load at the feet of Jesus, but we have got to leave it there, and know that He will help and direct us.

One reality God has shown me is that many times my prayer is answered, but I do not realize it. The problem is that I was not listening or watching for an answer. I have been guilty of making my request, and then just forgetting about it as if I really didn't expect it to happen anyway.

I must come to Jesus expecting an answer as Job did, and then I must be prepared to listen and wait. I must watch for signs of His response. The answer may not be exactly as I have anticipated, so I must be prepared for any sign of His response. When I have waited on God, I have not been disappointed in my request for an answer.

"Indeed, I know that this is true. But how can a mortal be righteous before God? Though one wished to dispute with him, he could not answer him one time out of a thousand. His wisdom is profound, his power is vast" (Job 9:2-3).

No one can dispute God and His wisdom and His authority! All His answers will be right and just!

Chapter 12

Modern Day Miracle
(Mid January 2006, I.U. Medical Center)

"Yum, chocolate!"

My mouth drooled as I popped open the tab and poked the straw down into the icy cold drink. I drew a very slow sip from the cup and held the liquid in my mouth. I savored the delicious taste and the little slivers of ice that filled my dry mouth.

"This can't be! It tastes so good. Thank You, Jesus, for this miracle! Praise Your Holy name!"

Who would have ever dreamed that God performed a miracle in me that allowed me to drink and eat? It's true and it was totally God! Despite what the surgeon told my family, and everyone else in the surgical waiting room, only a week after my surgery I was allowed to have liquids! It was an absolute miracle straight from God to me! "Thank You, Jesus!" Dr. Touloukian started me out on ice chips and then I graduated to Boost, a nutritional drink supplement. It was chocolate and tasted just like a milkshake! What a wonderful blessing!

Two weeks later, I was eating a soft diet, and the following week I was allowed solids! I literally ate solid food only four weeks after a major surgery that the surgeon never expected me to survive! My family was warned several times that I might never eat again, and I cannot stress how much of a miracle it was for me to be drinking and eating!

I remembered my surgeon's exact words, "You will likely never eat again."

I heard it, but I didn't hear it. I believe God shielded me from ever internalizing that message, because I never believed that I would not eat again. I just knew the day would come when Dr. Touloukian would allow me to eat, and that was that!

When Dr. Touloukian told Larry and me that I would be starting on liquids and eventually solids, only one week after surgery, we were stunned, because I never imagined it would be this soon. Naturally, we were both curious as to how the surgeon came to the decision to let me drink, and eventually eat, when he was dead set against it earlier. The surgeon explained. "When a patient has bowel surgery a major concern is that the bowel might not 'wake up' or begin to function again."

Since my admission and surgery at I.U. Medical Center on January 8th, 2006, and including my previous days at Decatur County Memorial Hospital, it had been over three weeks since I'd had any liquids by mouth, and over a month since I'd eaten food. My bowel did not work this entire time, and I had undergone three separate bowel surgeries at that point. Dr. Touloukian said my body needed to at least go through the motions of processing food, even if the food didn't stay in my system and I didn't retain any nutrients. The longer the surgeon waited to introduce liquids and food, the harder it would be for my bowel to resume digestion, and if he didn't introduce liquids or foods soon to stimulate the bowel, the bowel might never "wake up." In fact, the bowel could even die.

Oh, yes, there were serious risks in allowing me to drink and eat. The most obvious risk was the possibility of the tissue-thin bowel not being able to handle the digestion process, so the bowel might rupture. However, Dr. Touloukian really wanted to try to give me the absolute best shot possible at a normal life. I was so young, and my surgeon said he would never be able to forgive himself if he didn't at least let me try to drink and eat. If the bowel ruptured or other complications set in, we would deal with it then, but Dr. Touloukian felt he had to let me try, regardless of the risk. The Total Parental Nutrition supplement, or TPN, administered through my IV and which kept me alive, was loaded with calories and sugar. It was also keeping me from being hungry. He expected that eating and drinking would cause increased nausea and pain at first, and he was concerned that I might be afraid to eat. He wanted me to be able to eat in the worst way, and he stressed that I could not give up, no matter how much discomfort I might have. He really did care!

Dr. Touloukian continued, "Just take it very slow, and eat or drink very small amounts. The amount is not as important as it is just to drink or eat. You need to at least try. Do this for me, please. No, no. Do it for yourself! The worst thing that could happen is it doesn't work."

He called for a nurse to come and take out my NG tube. When I heard him talking to the nurse I was so thrilled! Yeah, I could have kissed him! I was so happy to get that tube out! Then the nurse brought me the icy cold, chocolate Boost drink. I was extremely nervous about taking that first sip, but in a matter of seconds that fear was completely gone. Before I knew it, I was drinking, and eventually I was eating. Eating! Praise the Lord, a miracle occurred! I loved being able to eat and drink, but there was a dreadful cost. I vomited everything I ate! It took a long time for my body to learn to digest food, even the smallest amounts. All the wrenching was so painful, especially with my open wound. My abdominal muscles were so sore, and my esophagus was raw from all the vomiting. What really encouraged me to keep trying to eat was the fact that my taste buds were working perfectly! Everything tasted so good! The sensation of eating, chewing food, and experiencing all the different food textures again was wonderful!

Praise God, digesting food was not too much stress on the bowel, and I didn't have any ruptures. A flood of delicious memories associated with eating food came over me. Food was such a comfort to me. Believe it or not, it was more than worth all the vomiting just to be able to enjoy eating again. I prayed that the vomiting would stop or slow down very quickly, because if it didn't, the surgeon would put the NG tube back in and I sure didn't want that!

Eventually, the vomiting did slow and the colostomy began working effectively, too. I was not absorbing any nutrients from the liquids or food I was eating, because everything I took in went straight through me and directly to my colostomy bag. It didn't stay in my system long enough to digest, so I had to stay on the TPN.

The nurses gave me TPN three times a day through my IV, and it kept me alive. For that, I was very thankful. The down side to TPN is that it is so concentrated it can actually do damage to the liver and other organs if it is taken over a long period of time.

I was on the TPN for over a year, and I do have some slight liver damage. My liver enzymes continue to rise, but there is no imminent danger of liver failure, and no other organs seem to have been affected. I have thanked God many times over for Dr. Touloukian and for his excellent care.

Job knew the mighty power of God and He understood that only God could perform a miracle to cure him and bring back his joy.

"He alone stretches out the heavens and treads on the waves of the sea. He is the Maker of the Bear and Orion, the Pleiades and the constellations of the south. He performs wonders that cannot be fathomed, miracles that cannot be counted. When he passes me, I cannot see him; when he goes by, I cannot perceive him. If he snatches away, who can stop him; ..." (Job 9:8-11).

God is just in His dealings with man, and Job longed to be exonerated. Job was continually accused by his friends of having unconfessed sin, and this was his punishment for that sin. Job did not know of any such sin in his life, but the more beaten down he became, the more he began to believe his friends' accusations, and he begged God to reveal the sin if there was one. Job knew in his heart that God would bring his faithfulness to light, and he knew God would eventually show his friends that they were wrong about him.

"Oh, that my words were recorded, that they were written on a scroll, that they were inscribed with an iron tool on lead, or engraved in rock forever! I know that my Redeemer lives, and that in the end he will stand upon the earth. And after my skin has been destroyed, yet in my flesh I will see God; I myself will see him with my own eyes – I, and not another. How my heart yearns within me!" (Job 19:23-27).

Job never lost sight of God's ability to clear his name, to give him a miracle of renewed health, and to have his joy restored. What he didn't know was whether the miracle would be here on earth or in heaven. When would he see God with his own eyes?

After a time, God did give Job a miracle. He prospered Job and gave him twice as much as he had before. In the latter part of Job's life, God presented Job with thousands of animals, seven sons, and three beautiful daughters and allowed him to live to be 140 years of age. He saw his children and their children to the fourth generation!

God blessed Job for his faithfulness and for the fact that in all of Job's adversities, he remained blameless. Yes, Job was blessed with a miracle of vindication, and a life of sheer joy and unbelievable success, and God did a miracle in me, too! Dr. Touloukian did what he was trained to do, but my body was in such a fragile state that only God could bring it back to a point that I would not only live, but I would also be able to eat!

God is so GOOD ALL THE TIME! He has done many miracles in my life, but my complete healing is yet to be seen. Like Job, I don't know if my miracle of complete physical healing will be here on earth or in heaven. Either way, I will trust in Him, because I know my Jesus will heal me. He wants the absolute best for me, and I will wait upon Him. His timing is perfect!

I know my Redeemer lives, and I pray that I will never charge God with wrongdoing, and that my heart will always yearn and strive to be blameless in His sight, as with Job. Job encourages me to keep going, to remain firm in what I believe, and to keep my heart, mind and eyes focused on Jesus.

Chapter 13

The Hands and Feet of Christ
(Mid January 2006, I.U. Medical Center)

I remember a moment that forever changed the life of my roommate. My roommate had a serious infection which destroyed much of her right arm and shoulder. Her entire right arm and shoulder were bandaged, leaving only the tips of her fingers exposed. She was in horrible pain, and she couldn't even sleep in a bed, so she slept in a recliner the entire time we were together. At meal time, a nurse had to help feed her, or she would try to eat with her left hand. When she fed herself, she ate very little, and she wore more food than she ate. She couldn't keep the food on her fork or get the food to her mouth. It was difficult to watch, and many times I prayed a nurse would help her. Sometimes a nurse would help, and sometimes not. It really made me sad. The nurses rely heavily on family members to help with patient care. It's not right, but that's how it is, because they are short-staffed and can only do so much.

My roommate rarely got a full bath because she did not have family members there to help her. Her family lived over two hours away, and her husband could not miss work, so they came mostly on the weekends. She had been in the hospital over a month already before I came.

One particular morning, I was feeling especially low. I hadn't had a decent bath in several days myself, my hair was matted and greasy, and I really needed a boost. I knew Anna was coming to visit, and I asked her if she could bring some good smelling shampoo and lotions and help me with a bath.

A couple of hours later Anna showed up with two of my sisters-in-law, Patti and Gloria, and a friend, Michelle. The four ladies began to do their magic. They washed my hair, gave me a thorough cleaning from head to toe, helped me brush my teeth, trimmed my fingernails and toenails, shaved my legs, massaged me with lotion, and styled my hair. I felt like a princess, and it was wonderful! Wow, it was as if I'd been to a spa!

As they began to clean up the towels and put their supplies away, I looked over at my roommate, my friend. My roommate was talking and laughing with us the entire time I was enjoying my bath, and she seemed to love my family. I always included her in visits with family or friends.

Now she looked at me with the most longing eyes. "I haven't had my hair washed in weeks. Do you think your family would wash my hair, too?" she asked.

I could have cried. Here I was receiving so much love and attention while she watched silently, hoping all along that she, too, could have some small manner of help, even if it was just to get her hair washed. I felt horrible!

Before I could respond, the four ladies picked up and moved to her bedside. I know they were a little fearful and concerned about the possibility of her infection spreading, but God worked in them. They showed her no signs of fear, and they did for her all the wonderful treatments they did for me, including shaving her legs!

This was the most selfless act of discipleship – being the "hands and feet of Christ" – I have ever experienced. My roommate was brought to tears with gratitude. Many times after that she mentioned to me how much she loved my family, and how no one ever did anything like that for her before. She saw Jesus with skin on!

I have spent hundreds of hours in hospitals, and I usually had a roommate. It became apparent to me early on that God allowed these special opportunities for me to witness about Him and to be an encouragement to the new friends I met. Likewise, I was always blessed to know them and to share our time together.

"Think how you have instructed many; how you have strengthened feeble hands. Your words have supported those who stumbled; you have strengthened faltering knees. But now trouble comes to you, and you are discouraged; it strikes you and you are dismayed. Should not your piety be your confidence and your blameless ways your hope?" (Job 4:3-6). Job must have had many friends in days gone by. Maybe the majority of people Job

thought were friends were really mere acquaintances. There is a big difference between an acquaintance and a friend. Where was everyone? Job was in big trouble and only three people show up? He was a very prominent businessman; he'd helped many people, and had a big family. What's the deal?

The three men who came to be with Job considered themselves to be Job's friends, but they were only acquaintances. As they talked to Job the three men tried to explain to him why Job might have caused his own predicament. The more the three men tried to help, the more accusatory they became. Okay, so they were pious, and they did come across pretty harsh at times, but they still believed they were helping Job. They believed it was their duty to be a "priest" to Job.

Job challenged his "so called" friends. *"How you have helped the powerless! How you have saved the arm that is feeble! What advice you have offered to one without wisdom! And what great insight you have displayed! Who has helped you utter these words? And whose spirit spoke from your mouth?" (Job 26:1-4).*

It would be easy for me to avoid my discipleship responsibilities by reasoning that I don't want to offend someone, I'm not professionally trained, and I'm not a pastor. Still, Christians are "called" to be priests to all believers. It's my duty to encourage and pray for those in need, to be a help where I can. When I do go out in the name of Christ, I must be prepared to serve Him and to GO armed with God's Word – not my words.

When I pray about a situation and ask God to guide me and give me the words to speak, He does. It is amazing how much better I feel when I take my eyes off myself and do for others. I find I am blessed just for being a blessing. When I think about the problems that led to my being in the hospital, I can't help but think about the blessings that resulted from that hospitalization. The blessings have far outweighed the troubles.

Chapter 14

Pure Torture (Late January 2006, I.U. Medical Center)

One day a nurse came to my room and said, "We need to take you down to X-ray for a new test your surgeon ordered. The surgeon wants to see how bad your bowel leaks are." My brother Jim had come to visit me, and he hadn't even been there five minutes before the nurse came in, and I didn't want him to leave. I asked the nurse how long the X-ray would take, and she said it would involve a half hour to an hour at the most. So, I asked Jim to come with me to the X-ray department and wait for me there, and I was never so thankful that he was with me as I was that day. It ended up that the test lasted a couple of hours! Those two hours were the most horrendous and painful hours of my time in the hospital. It was pure torture!

In the X-ray department the technicians gave me eight-ounce glasses of thick, white, chalky barium to drink. They filled my small bowel with barium through the colostomy, and they filled the lower eighteen-inch section of colon with barium. My stomach and every inch of my colon were filled with barium, and I felt like my body was blown up to twice my normal size. It was very painful, and I thought I was going to explode. I was already very nauseated and experiencing frequent vomiting with any drinking or eating.

The technicians had me lying on a very cold, hard metal table with no pillow and no blanket. Then they took pictures of me lying flat, lying on each side, and standing. Every twenty minutes they repeated the hideous procedure.

When I could not drink any more barium and vomited it up, they just gave me more. If I lost any barium through my stoma or bowel, they just filled it up again. I was in excruciating pain!

After the first couple of rounds of X-rays, my gown was soaked in vomit. I was freezing! That, along with having to twist and turn all over the place on the cold metal table, nearly did me in.

I tried so hard not to cry, but occasionally tears streamed down my cheeks. I was shaking so badly I could hardly lie still, and I was so cold that my teeth were chattering. I asked for a clean gown, and the X-ray techs gave me one, but it wasn't long before that one was also covered in vomit. I can't express how horrible it was to lie there soaked in vomit, freezing, twisting and turning like a pretzel, and feeling like every inch of my body could "blow out" at any moment!

The X-ray techs felt terrible for me, and they began to apologize. They asked the radiologist if they could cut back on the amount of barium I was forced to drink, but he denied the request because the test would not be effective without the proper amount of barium, and he needed to see every part of my small bowel and colon.

That did it! I broke out in inconsolable sobbing. This was absolute torture! Nobody should have to endure this! No one! I prayed they would stop. After each set of pictures I asked for a cold, wet rag to wipe the taste of vomit from my mouth. The techs set a huge stack of cold, wet rags on the table next to my head, so I had one whenever I needed it.

To this day, I don't know what kept me on that table. I believe that God had angels holding me there and helping me to make it through. Finally, the last sets of pictures were taken. Thank God! The techs helped me off the table and sent me to the bathroom to clean up. They also gave me another clean gown. They didn't realize how sick I was, and I had no idea how I was going to clean myself up. The moment the bathroom door closed behind me I could feel the room spinning, and I tried to reach for the cord on the wall to call for help. I couldn't reach it, so I leaned back against the wall to keep from falling and slowly slid down to the floor. When I didn't come out from the bathroom after several minutes, the techs came to check on me. I was still in my vomit soaked gown, sitting on the cold tile floor, leaned up against the wall. I was too weak to move. They called for help, and they got me up and onto a cart. They cleaned me up and changed my gown.

I asked for a warm blanket and an X-ray tech came back with a sheet. A sheet? Really? I'm freezing to death and all I got was a thin little sheet? Did anyone care how I felt? Did anyone have a clue how badly I just wanted to die? The techs wheeled me into the hallway to wait for the transport team to take me back to my room, and Jim came from the waiting area and stood with me there. I was crying as I tried to tell him what happened. Before I could finish, the X-ray girls were back, and they were obviously disturbed. "We are sorry, but the last set of pictures did not take. The radiologist said we have to repeat the last set of pictures." My heart stopped. I could tell they felt horrible about it, but nonetheless, I would have to drink more barium to repeat the pictures. I thought about it for a few seconds, and decided I would refuse. I had rights, and I would not let them torture me anymore! If they missed a few spots on the films, then so be it. I could not endure anymore, not one more drop of barium!

Jim was beside himself. He wanted so badly to help me, but he had no idea what to do. There was nothing he could do, but just having him there meant the world to me. The techs left me in the hallway with Jim while they got ready for the last few pictures. I was so glad they let him stay with me. I was at my very lowest point, and I prayed that God would take me right there and then!

I looked at Jim and said, "Jim, I am so tired. This has been horrible, and I can't take anymore. I am ready to go, I'm not afraid to go, and I hope I go very soon. I just want to go home. I love you so much, Jim." The look on his face was more than I could handle. He sobbed and gently stroked my legs. We could barely look at each other, and the slightest glance provoked more pain and more tears. Jim loves me so much, and I knew he was not ready for me to go, but I was.

The X-ray techs returned, and just the sight of them made my stomach churn. They wheeled me back into X-ray room to torture me one last time. I told them absolutely no more barium. I was going to vomit it up again anyway, so there was no point. They left for a few moments to talk to the radiologist.

When they came back they said, "Okay, here's the deal. If you will drink just half a glass of barium we can retake the last set of films. It has to stay down for at least five to seven minutes so we can get the pictures we need. Will you please try to drink just this much?"

I knew the techs felt intense pressure to make me drink the barium, but at this point, I really didn't care. I hesitated for a second as I looked at the glass of barium – I could feel the lump rising in my throat. Honestly, I did not know if I could keep it down for even ten seconds, so I mustered up the strength to say, "No, I can't do it. Sorry, but you'll have to take the pictures without it. I just won't do it. Tell that radiologist he can forget about any more pictures." Where did that come from? I didn't mean to be quite so harsh, but I was relieved that I had finally stood up for myself, and I was not going to have to drink any more barium.

I knew the radiologist was upset because I watched his face through the window as the techs explained my message. When they came back, to my surprise, they said, "Okay, we'll do it without the barium, but just know that the surgeon will not have all the pictures he needs."

"That's what they think! How dare they threaten me?" I was so angry in my spirit.

"God, please help me. Just take me home!"

I was afraid to respond, so I just prayed. I could feel my face flushing, and my eyes filled with tears. The radiologist proceeded to take four more pictures, and when they were through I was finally taken back to my room.

All the while, Jim never left my side. I wondered how I would ever have survived the ordeal without him. It was so comforting just to know he was right outside the X-ray room that whole time, praying for me. Once again, God extended His magnificent mercy and provided a blessing in the midst of a horrible storm.

"Do you have eyes of flesh? Do you see as a mortal sees? Are your days like those of a mortal or your years like those of a man, that you must search out my faults and probe after my sin – though you know that I am not guilty and that no one can rescue me from your hand? Your hands shaped me and made me. Will you now turn and destroy me?" (Job 10:4-8).

I learned that I can see myself as a victim, or I can be a vessel. Hum, victim versus vessel. What will it be? It's always easier to play the victim, and I do have lots of horror stories to share. I have every right to say I have been through a lot, but guess what? So have millions of others.

Job played the victim at times. *"Surely no one lays a hand on a broken man when he cries for help in his distress. Have I not wept for those in trouble? Has not my soul grieved for the poor? Yet when I hoped for good, evil came; when I looked for light, then came darkness" (Job 30:24-26).*

Job is having a bit of a pity party. He's completely honest regarding his feeling, yet he is not charging God. He is contrite, and he wants to make sure God knows how repulsive he feels.

I have been there, and I wondered if God had any clue how miserable I felt at times. It's honest, it's human, and it's where I was at the time. Yes, I have played the victim, but keeping my mind focused on God is certainly one way to turn that attitude around in a hurry. I can honestly say, despite all I've been through, I tried to move away from that victim emotion as soon as I recognized it. I want to be a usable vessel, because there is no peace or contentment in the victim mode.

Job also longed to be a usable vessel. *"... let God weigh me in honest scales, and he will know that I am blameless – if my steps have turned from the path, if my heart has been led by my eyes, or if my hands have been defiled, then may others eat what I have sown, and may my crops be uprooted" (Job 31:6-8).*

Job loved God and he would continue to do so, despite how his humanity betrayed him at times. Job was more interested in being the man God wanted him to be – a man of Godly character, and his desire was to be the vessel and not the victim. Enduring and surviving intense adversities can certainly encourage us to see the value of being a vessel for God.

I worry about my character, and I am keenly aware that it reflects my relationship with Jesus. I have grown in my faith, and I have come to know the value of being the usable vessel as well. If I remain the victim and let it be all about me, I will miss all the blessings of sharing Christ with the world – sharing His precious gift of salvation. God will only use me if I am willing to be used. It may not be in the fashion I envision, but He can still use me. I'm not perfect, and sometimes I find myself leaning towards that victim side, but Praise God, He helps me turn back. He allows me to see what He can do in me when I am the willing vessel.

Chapter 15

She's Going to Make It
(End of January 2006, I.U. Medical Center)

After a full month in the hospital, I showed signs of significant improvement. Since my admission to my local hospital, Decatur County Memorial, and having spent an additional month at I.U. Medical Center, I'd been in a hospital for over two months. That's a very long time!

One morning I was up earlier than usual after I endured another one of those sleepless nights in the hospital. Since I couldn't sleep, I figured I should go ahead and get cleaned up, and I called for the nurse. Taking a bath late in the day increased the chance of no hot, or even warm, water to bathe. I'd had plenty of cold baths while I was in the hospital, and I sure didn't want a cold bath this morning. I knew better than to expect anyone to help me this early in the morning and the nurse said she was okay with my getting a bath, but she confirmed that I'd have to do it on my own. I told her that was fine, so she got the basin of water ready for me and set the towels and other supplies on the side table, so I would have easy access to what I needed. Since this was my first attempt at a bath without any help, I really wanted to prove I could do it. My roommate was asleep, and I didn't have to worry about nurses coming and going or residents making rounds. I could take all the time I needed and not be interrupted.

I had no idea something so simple as bathing could cause so much pain and make me so weary. As I tried to reach all around to clean, I felt a burning in my gut. My incision was still very painful, and every move I made pulled on it. I took it slowly, very slowly, and after almost an hour I managed to hit all the vital areas. It felt so good to be clean, and I even managed to put lotion on my arms and legs. I was tired and hurting, but I was really proud of myself.

When the nurse came back to check on me she told me how proud she was of me, too. I told her I felt very refreshed, but I really wished I could have my legs shaved. Exhaustion took over, and I didn't know if I could even try. The nurse was very encouraging: "You can do it. Just try."

She got a razor and more lotion. My hands shook as I moved the razor up and down my leg. It felt so good just to shave my legs, and it felt even better knowing I could do it on my own!

Just as I finished my first leg, my surgeon ripped back the curtain! He scared me to death – no advance notice and no knock. How rude! What did he think he was doing? I almost gashed my leg! Really, 6 a.m. and the surgeon comes barging in with a great big smile as if I should have been expecting him, or be so thrilled to see him! Dr. Touloukian just stood there and stared at me. He looked at me for a few seconds with the funniest look on his face, and then he turned around and ran out like he'd just seen a ghost!

Evidently I really scared him, and that certainly didn't do much good for my self-esteem. I tried to understand what was going on, but I was determined to finish shaving before he pulled that little trick again.

As I expected, Dr. Touloukian was back in a couple of minutes; however, this time he brought three of his residents with him. Yes, I was still attempting to shave my leg. I don't know what was up with these surgeons and their lack of courtesy.

They all just stared at me for a moment and then broke out clapping. Clapping – now I was really confused, and I felt like a sideshow freak.

Then my surgeon said, "This is terrific! I wanted you doctors to see this because SHE is going to make it. People who are not going to make it DO NOT shave their legs. They physically can't, and they just don't care. She cares and she is going to make it!" My surgeon gave me a big high five and said, "Keep it up. You keep pushing and doing for yourself, and you'll be out of here very soon." I love Dr. Touloukian!

What a thrill to hear those words, and that was the boost I needed to keep me encouraged. I'd been hospitalized so … long and I really, I mean REALLY, wanted to go home. I believe that moment was a pivotal point in my recovery; I turned a corner and didn't look back. I continued to improve, and each day I got a little stronger.

The surgeon was true to his word. I had a long recovery ahead of me, but within a couple of weeks, Dr. Touloukian decided it was time for me to go home. A few days later, I lay back in my bed, and that whole scene where Dr. Touloukian told his residents I was "going to make it" played over and over in my head. I thought about how far I had come, and how I'd been through such ghastly situations, and survived! Glory to God for all that He has done in me. I attribute much of my strength to family and friends who continually prayed for me. They cheered me on and encouraged me in ways I never imagined, and they literally prayed and loved me back from the brink of death several times. I was never alone in my journey because God was always with me, and I had the added blessing of that enormous and strong support system.

Job was not so fortunate. His friends started out being supportive, but then they became indifferent to Job. When Job did not recover and his situation got worse, his friends began to question and accuse him.

"Submit to God and be at peace with him; in this way prosperity will come to you. Accept instruction from his mouth and lay up his words in your heart. If you return to the Almighty, you will be restored: ..." (Job 22:21-23).

"How long will you torment me and crush me with words? Ten times now you have reproached me; shamelessly you attack me" (Job 19:2-3).

Job's "so called" friends did not let up. They truly believed Job suffered so much because he had wickedness in his heart; he sinned against God, and Job's friends felt they needed to prove a point. How painful for Job to be constantly judged, and how did Job hold up under the condemnation, and where did he find the strength to be faithful? Job's faith was firmly planted in God. He may not have understood God's ways, but he knew better than to turn away from God, and he did not look to man to save him. He would have loved to have had the support of friends, but he saw firsthand how fickle man was and how quickly they turned against him. God was everything to Job and all he had, so Job placed all his hope in God.

"But he knows the way that I take; when he has tested me, I will come forth as gold. My feet have closely followed his steps; I have kept to his way without turning aside. I have not departed from the commands of his lips; I have treasured the words of his mouth more than my daily bread" (Job 23:10-12).

Job could stand up under such grueling circumstances because he walked daily with God. Job treasured the words of God's mouth more than food, and Job's eyes were on God because Job's hope was in Him. Job's focus was on God alone.

Many times I, too, long for the words of Jesus, and His words are sweet as honey and as refreshing as cool, clean water. I depend on His Word to keep me going, and I am reminded of His promises and His deep love for me. That is how I endure and how I keep coming back to Jesus. I can't allow myself to be away from Him for very long, or I start to stray and question. Jesus provides all the answers I need, and in Him I am able to withstand all that comes against me.

I do appreciate the Body of Christ and others who supported me throughout the years more than they'll ever know, but ultimately, God sustains me and delivers me. We humans try, as best we can, not to fail, but it is impossible. At some point, our flesh will fail us, we'll make mistakes, let people down, and even let God down. The only certainty anyone can count on is God!

Chapter 16

Going Home (February 2006, I.U. Medical Center)

Word spread quickly that I was coming home. Everyone was excited, but no one more than I! I received calls from people welcoming me home before I was even officially discharged! Good news travels fast! Larry was gone from home so much that I expected the house to be in shambles. My personality would not allow me a moment's peace until the house was picked up and cleaned. Okay, I am OCD, I have been for years; Larry knew this, so he made a phone call to some friends for help.

My Sunday School class from church was more than willing to help. They, along with a few other friends from church, went to our home the day before I was released from the hospital and gave it a thorough cleaning. They put fresh sheets on the beds and made sure the entire place was perfect. They even did all the laundry because they didn't want me to have to worry about anything when I got home. I couldn't wait to get home and dive into my own bed and nice clean sheets!

Praise the Lord, after nearly ten weeks in the hospital I was going home: home to my own place, my little family, and my feisty little dog, Annie. I was far from healed, but coming home was a huge step in my journey to wellness.

I was sent home, having a huge open wound that was now about seven inches in length and every bit of four inches deep in one place, a colostomy, IV fluids for hydration, TPN for nutrition, and IV antibiotics. I still had my Wound Vac and continued to have the Wound Vac for another three months, and then on and off for another year. A home health nurse came to my home three times a week for nursing care and for teaching, so I could learn to do as much of my own care as possible.

The powerful antibiotics were very hard on my stomach, so

I was given medications to help with the nausea, but many times I vomited, and when I did, it was murderous on my incision! Vomiting, coughing, or even sneezing brought about terrible pain, and I still had the two fistulas. While I was in the hospital, and even after I'd been home, I had several surgical procedures to close both fistulas, but none were effective. Infection flowed freely through the fistulas and continued to cause intense pain in my tailbone, low back, and lower abdomen. A Jackson Pratt drainage pouch was put in to contain the drainage from the fistula on my abdomen, and wound packing and bandage changes still needed to be done every three days. Each time the tape was removed, it felt like a layer of skin was removed, too. At times I could barely tolerate the dressing changes. The nurses tried different ointments and powders to heal the patches of missing skin, but the packing and taping continued. On top of all of this, I grew more and more internal adhesions. The adhesions pulled and irritated my abdominal organs, and they still do. With every surgery new adhesions develop and even the attempt to remove the adhesions creates new ones.

My prayers for going home finally materialized, but I still faced difficulties. Nevertheless, I thanked God repeatedly for His great love and mercy, and for bringing me through all that I had endured. I finally made it home!

"How I long for the months gone by, for the days when God watched over me, when his lamp shone upon my head and by his light I walked through darkness! Oh, for the days when I was in my prime, when God's intimate friendship blessed my house, when the Almighty was still with me and my children were around me, when my path was drenched with cream and the rock poured out for me streams of olive oil" (Job 29:2-6).

When I got home I wanted everything to be back to "normal" – as it used to be, and I wanted my old life back. Still, I had reservations and I wasn't sure if I wanted to continue to run my life as I had for so many years. I'd made a lot of mistakes and the possibility of starting over was tempting, but not exactly exciting.

I knew I could not go back, and yet I didn't know how to move forward. I guess I just wanted some sense of normalcy in my life. Home was familiar and it was a place of safety and wonderful memories. I trusted that God would get me through, just as He had so many times before. New and exciting changes would come for me, and yet I just wanted to be back with my family, for us to be okay financially, and my new relationship with Jesus to flourish. My relationship with Jesus had slowly developed to a point that I realized the more I leaned on Him, the more I needed Him. He was all I needed, and when my heart was right with God everything else in my life followed suit. The financial security, my job and all the other responsibilities that I deemed so important were all questionable, and I didn't know if any of it would be there now, but that was okay; I had Jesus and He was enough. I knew my life would be different – better than anything I had ever known before, and I trusted that the best was yet to come.

Chapter 17

The Rubber Meets the Road (February 2006, Home)

My first day home I was thrilled to learn my home health nurse was a previous co-worker and friend. Debbie works for Decatur County Home Health, and she was familiar with my history, she knew my disposition, and she knew how important God and family are to me. Of all the nurses I could have had, I got her. I couldn't wait to see her once I knew she was the one who would be coming. Debbie showed up a couple of hours after I got home. I was already overwhelmed from the trip home, and I wanted nothing more than to lie down. I opted for the couch so I wouldn't have to get up out of bed when she came. When Debbie walked in, she immediately came to me and gave me the biggest hug ever! Thank You, Jesus, for Debbie.

Debbie understood how overwhelmed I was. She was very compassionate, but she was also very firm. She said I would be taking a long, hard journey, but she had no doubt that I would be up to the challenge. I believe she knew my capabilities better than I did as she began to unveil the plan, the big, long, hard plan. I slowly saw that my care at home would be a monstrous job and that's where the rubber meets the road!

After three hours of new patient admission paperwork, then the exam, the explanation of how to administer my IV antibiotics and fluids, and how to care for my colostomy, I reached my limit. I was tired, in tears, hurting, and scared. Before I could stop myself, I looked at Debbie and blurted out, "I am not a nurse! I did not sign up for this, and I can't do it! I thought you were here to do this, so why do I have to do this when I can't even hold my head up? I am exhausted, and I need help! Isn't that what you are here for?"

It was too late. The words were said, and I couldn't take them back. I was so ashamed at my behavior, but it was how I really felt.

I loved Debbie and I would never have purposely hurt her, but I really meant what I'd said. She looked at me with much compassion, and she did not scold me for my harsh remarks. Instead, she hugged me, smiled at me, and slowly began helping me start my IV and antibiotics. I could feel my hurt and anger slowly melt away. When we finally finished, I stood up to go to bed. I could finally go to bed! I was careful to get up and not to make any quick moves because every move was painful, so I didn't mind taking it slowly. Larry bent down to move my IV tubing so I wouldn't trip over it. As I moved past him, he noticed something wet on his shoulder.

"What's this?" he said.

My sister Anna realized right away what it was. She tried to say it as nicely as possible as she pointed to my colostomy bag. I was horrified to find my colostomy bag was leaking! I was so embarrassed, and felt so bad for him.

He just stood up and said, "It's alright. It washes off."

Then he cracked a big smile and began to laugh. That is why I love him so much! One at a time, others in the room joined in the laughter, and before I knew it, I was laughing, too. We eventually made our way to the bedroom, and I was never so glad to get in bed and press my head into my own pillow. Debbie helped me to get settled into bed before she left, and I asked Debbie for forgiveness for my harsh words to her, but, to this day, she says she does not remember any harsh words spoken to her. God is so good to shield us, and those we love, from remembering hurtful words we say and the deeds we do.

Finally, everyone left the house. Only Anna and Larry remained, and I reflected on the day and said my prayers. I never in a million years dreamed that I would be in this situation at this very moment. How did this happen? I was still trying to figure out why and what it all meant for my future, and for the future of my family.

All of a sudden I felt that all too familiar wetness flow all down my side and onto the clean bedding. I yelled for Anna and Larry. They came running and checked out the bandages. Sure enough, my colostomy was leaking all over the place. The only option was to change it, but the nurse just left – we needed to try it by ourselves. Larry and Anna would not let me get discouraged.

"We'll do it. We have to do it by ourselves sometime anyway. We can do it," they said.

I was confident they could change it, and I really had no other choice, so I just let them go at it. It was difficult to trust any non-medical person completely with my care, and this was the moment of truth! I was sent home from the hospital with two complete colostomy appliance changes. Larry and Anna took the old appliance off without much trouble, but ruined the seal on the Wound Vac in the process. I was confident they could change the colostomy, but getting the Wound Vac changed and sealed was a whole new issue. Again, I had to trust. We managed to get the new flange on, and it seemed to be sealed; now we just needed to attach the bag. Anna tried to snap the bag on and struggled, so Larry took a shot at it, but he was unsuccessful, too. Great! Something was terribly wrong. It was then they discovered the mistake: they finally realized the bag was a different size from the flange! It works like Tupperware. In order for the lid to seal, it must be a perfect match to the bowl, or in this case, the flange!

Oh, my! I was hysterical. I managed to hold myself together pretty well all day, and then I endured the grueling three hours of training, and now this! Liquid stool just kept pouring out, and I just started sobbing. I wanted to be strong for my family, but I was failing miserably. I think it was the first time in a long time they saw me cry.

Anna looked at me and said, "I don't care if I have to drive all the way back to Indianapolis. I will find a bag that fits TONIGHT! Do you hear me? We will fix this!"

I love Anna so much. She called the home health nurse to explain the situation, met her at their office, and the two of them spent almost an hour going through random colostomy supplies looking for perfect matches. Finally, they found a couple of sets that matched and Anna came home with the new supplies. Anna got right to work and, within an hour or so, she had the colostomy system in place, and the Wound Vac resealed. Praise the Lord!

I was so exhausted! I don't remember getting up even once

to go to the bathroom that night. I sure hoped Anna was able to get some rest because I knew she was past the point of exhaustion as well. I'm sure poor Larry didn't sleep, because he was the one that emptied my colostomy bag all night while I slept, God bless him.

"You gave me life and showed me kindness, and in your providence watched over my spirit" (Job 10:12).

Job loved and feared God. God blessed Job, and he'd always lived a very prosperous life. He never struggled as he did now, and he would rely on his understanding of who God was and the fact that God never failed him. He did not take lightly the promises of God and He knew whatever God did, or allowed, it was right, and God was in it. Job didn't understand, but he was in this for the duration. He had no idea what else might happen to him or how long his misery might go on, but it didn't matter, because Job was determined to be faithful till the end.

"... as long as I have life within me, the breath of God in my nostrils, my lips will not speak wickedness, and my tongue will utter no deceit. I will never admit you are in the right; till I die, I will not deny my integrity. I will maintain my righteousness and never let go of it; my conscience will not reproach me as long as I live" (Job 27:3-6).

I never struggled as I did now, and I had to rely on my understanding of who God is and in the fact that God had never failed me. I did not take lightly the promises of God. I learned that whatever God did, or allowed, it was right, and God was in it. I didn't always understand, but I was in this for the duration. I had no idea what else might happen to me, or how long my misery might go on. It didn't matter, because I wanted to be faithful till the end.

Oh, I was tempted at times to give up on God. Yes, I was mad and I cried out to God.

"Why is this happening? What did I do to deserve this? I thought You were a God of love!"

I could have succumbed to the lies of Satan and been so angry and bitter regarding all the horrible problems in my life, but I had the Holy Spirit, the very Spirit of God, deep within me. God did not allow those evil thoughts to take root in my mind or in my heart.

Chapter 18

The Blessing of Friends and Family
(Feb. through Oct. 2006, Home)

My family made arrangements prior to my release from the hospital for me to have the twenty-four hour care seven days a week that I needed. Larry had to get back to work, and Meg and Sam were still in college and could not miss any more school. Each one of my brothers and sisters took turns staying with me during the day and through the night. Some of my sisters-in-law, and even brothers-in-law helped, too. Even a couple of my nieces stayed with me.

It was a huge sacrifice for all to be away from their own families, and especially for them to stay with me not knowing what crisis might occur, or what mess they might have to clean up on their shift. None of them made me feel guilty about keeping them away from their family or job. They loved me and willingly helped, no matter how difficult it was. As my family began to wear down, church friends were added to the care-giving list.

My niece Amy is an EMT (Emergency Medical Technician), and she was more than willing to help. I needed someone to learn to take care of the Wound Vac and to be available on the days when the home health nurses weren't there. There were not many people who could stomach the dressing changes and wound care of my massive open wound, but Amy could. There were several times when I had problems with the Wound Vac, and I had to call her. It seemed many of my problems occurred on the weekends. Amy has two children and is a very busy mom and I hated bothering her on the weekends, but she was so kind to come every time. I was so thankful for her help, and she was so tender and loving with me. Being in bed, flat on my back most of the time, only intensified my back pain. My back ached all the time, and Amy seemed to have the magic touch for alleviating the pain, even if the relief only lasted for a short time.

Those were the times that Amy and I shared our struggles, and we prayed together. Caregiving is so much more than the physical care, and for me the emotional and spiritual care is just as important as the physical. As much of a blessing that Amy was for me, I believe that I was a blessing to her as well. God used my situation to bring Amy and me much closer.

Michelle, a friend and nurse, was also a huge encouragement to me. Michelle is one of those people who can really boost one's confidence so the patient aspires to reach their full potential. She is full of life and an achiever! She is an exceptional lady, and I feel so fortunate to have her help and friendship.

I had a very difficult time getting out of bed and to the bathroom. With my large abdominal wound, two bags attached to my abdomen, IV tubing, and the Wound Vac machine to maneuver, I was frazzled and very frustrated. My bathroom was only about six feet from my bed, but I was still very uneasy about making it another six feet to the toilet. I became very dependent on my family to help me get there, and I even considered having a potty chair beside my bed. As I look back, I realize now that I was too dependent on others for most of my care. I didn't see it at the time, but Michelle did.

It was high time I started doing more for myself, but I needed a little push to get there, and Michelle was just the person to help me make the transition. She was very understanding, but she was also very firm. As long as I was willing to do the hard work, Michelle did whatever was necessary to help me heal, and be more independent. She would not allow me to give into fear or frustration. She was so passionate that she even had me believing I could be independent again, and she made sure I had every opportunity and resource to make that happen.

One night while Michelle stayed with me, she sat down on the side of the bed and chattered for awhile. It wasn't long before we talked about how my physical condition bothered me and my fear of taking some of my medications. One of my evening medications made me feel very woozy. Michelle listened intently as I shared my concerns, and she understood why I was so perturbed. She offered some insight as to why the medications were ordered, and why it was important to take them as directed. She also offered to get some additional supplies and IV tubing to make my transfer to the bathroom easier.

As promised, bright and early the very next day, Michelle showed up at my home with the extended tubing for my IV. She helped me situate myself in bed so I could get up and walk to the bathroom without getting tangled in all the tubing or falling. Michelle was extremely patient with me, and she continued coaching and cheering me on as I moved slowly from the bed to the bathroom. After a few minutes, I made it to the bathroom. Yeah, I did it and it felt so good to know I could get to the bathroom on my own. Michelle caused me to push myself and regain some of my independence! To make the victory even sweeter, she celebrated with me! She knew how badly I needed that encouragement, and she did not disappoint me. God knew I needed Michelle, and I was very blessed to have her love and support.

My friend Teresa is a wonderful organizer, and she is full of energy. I was excited to see what the night would bring when she was scheduled to stay with me. She is very caring, and she loves to find ways to make people feel better and feel loved. I had a hospital side table sitting beside the couch that another friend had loaned to me, so I could have my supplies close at hand. Since it was on wheels, I could wheel it down the hallway at night, and park it beside my bed. Before I knew it, the table teemed with important gadgets that seemed to constantly fall off or get in the way when I searched for space to put my plate or glass. I needed a way to organize all the little tubes of medications, Kleenex, cards, my Bible, pens, paper, and my phone.

Teresa was up to the challenge, and she purchased a rubber shelf mat. She cut the mat down to size, and placed it on the table. Then she set the stackable trays and containers she'd purchased on top of the mat to organize all the supplies. Everything I needed was close at hand, and that freed up a lot of space. I had more than enough room for a plate, space to write letters, or to set my Bible. Teresa's system also took care of the problem of items falling off the table or sliding around. It felt really good to have all the clutter organized.

Teresa looked for a trash can, and couldn't believe I didn't have one by my table. I didn't want an actual trash can sitting beside the table, because it was just one more obstacle to maneuver around when I got up. Also, I feared my tubing and cords might get tangled around a trash can. I really did need one for the soiled gloves, bandages, used medication supplies and other trash, but there was just no good place for it. Teresa agreed that a trash can was a hazard, and she came up with a brilliant idea. It was so simple! She taped a brown paper lunch bag to the side of my table. When the bag was filled we just threw it away and taped a new bag to the table. It sounds so simple, but it was a really big deal!

Next, Teresa helped me organize kits that included all the supplies I needed for the different IV infusions scheduled throughout the day. Four times a day I infused different antibiotics, and it was extremely difficult to keep track of the timing and the different supplies needed for each infusion. Teresa used gallon-sized Ziploc bags to organize the supplies, and each bag also contained the antibiotic, except for the ones that needed to be refrigerated. Rubber gloves, syringes, IV tubing, needles, connectors, saline, heparin, alcohol pads, and batteries for the IV pump were easily accessible. A label on the outside of the bag indicated the antibiotic, date, and time of infusion. When I was ready for the next infusion, my caregivers could pull out a bag and have everything they needed. That was a huge help, and it made life for me and all my caregivers so much easier.

Teresa is a marvelous friend, and I don't think she ever realized how those simple helps improved my life. God just kept putting incredible people in my life who made the recovery process so much better, and Teresa was one of those very special people! I was so blessed to have her then, and I am still blessed to have her in my life today!

Sunday School classes at church, my co-workers, and friends sent daily meals for our family and the caregivers. When I needed help, it was there. Different people throughout the community made sure my daily needs were met, and I felt like the most blessed person in the world. Actually, I WAS one of the most blessed people in the world right then. God saw to it that my every need was met.

One Christmas Eve, Larry got a call from our friends Brian and Susan. They wanted to bring over something for Larry and me. I told Larry that I thought they were bringing over Brian's famous cinnamon rolls. My mouth began to water, just thinking about those rolls. Fortunately, I was totally wrong about the cinnamon rolls.

A few days earlier I had talked with my friend Brian on the phone. He was checking to see how well I was doing. In the conversation, he asked about what I was able to do, and how I spent my days. I told Brian that I enjoyed surfing the Internet and reading and sending e-mails, but I didn't get to use our computer since I couldn't sit at my computer desk in the kitchen for any length of time. I was in bed most of the time, so Larry and I considered the possibility of getting a laptop computer in the spring. Our conversation switched to other thoughts, and we talked for several more minutes. Brian is a very good friend, and it is amazing how he always seems to call or e-mail at just the right time.

When Brian and his wife, Susan, showed up at our home that Christmas Eve, they were carrying a very large, heavy box wrapped in beautiful paper. I couldn't imagine what was in the package, but as I started to pull off the wrapping, I could see a box with a picture of a computer. I was even more thrilled that it was a laptop computer! What a wonderful gift! I never expected to be blessed with such an amazing gift, nor did I realize at the time what an impact the laptop computer would have in my life, but God did. Larry and I were overcome with emotion and fought back tears.

Then Brian shared how God gave him the idea for the computer. "After our conversation the other day, I felt God leading me to buy you a laptop. I did not know how I was going to pay for it, especially now at Christmas. Susan and I hadn't even finished shopping for our own children. I began to pray about it, and in a matter of minutes, God gave me the idea that I should ask several friends to help. If twenty-five friends each gave ten dollars, I could buy the laptop I saw advertised in a local flyer just a couple of days ago. I called the store and talked to someone in the electronics department to see if they had any of the computers left, and they had one left! They said that they would hold it for me. I immediately got on the phone and made a few calls. Then I sent out a mass e-mail, and within half an hour, I had all the money promised that I needed to get the computer. I even had a little extra so you can buy some additional programs if you want."

We were just amazed, and we could not believe the generosity and love of all those people who did this for me. I remember Brian saying that he knew I was to have the laptop, and that he knew I would use it to glorify God. I believed I would use it for that purpose, too, but I had no idea just how vital this laptop would be in allowing me to share Christ in the way He has allowed! God had all the details worked out to provide the avenue I needed to share Him with the locals, those living outside of our community and even those living outside of the United States. God's love reaches from the heavens and extends to the entire world!

I used the laptop to initiate a CHRISTmas program our church implemented two years ago. It is the laptop used to receive thousands of inspiring e-mails from family and friends from all over the United States that encouraged me to keep the faith and never give up. I used the same laptop to write "updates" informing family and friends of my condition. In all my medical adversities my journey with God has been my consolation, and I have used this laptop to write several blogs journaling some of the incredible blessings and insights that God has shown me along the way. This laptop was also used to write this book! To say this laptop has been a blessing is an understatement! This laptop has made a profound difference in my life as it has been used in many situations to serve God, to honor Him, and to share praises of all that God has done in and for me. God is so…….GOOD! How very blessed I have been to have such loving and amazing friends!

Even the one Job loved turned against him. Job's only living family member, his wife, wanted nothing to do with him; in fact, Job's wife wanted him to curse God and die! No one, absolutely no one, wanted to be around Job. Everyone just vanished, and Job was left to care for himself. He must have felt total abandonment; still, Job did not sin against God.

"He has alienated my brothers from me; my acquaintances are completely estranged from me. My kinsmen have gone away; my friends have forgotten me. My guests and my maidservants count

me a stranger; they look upon me as an alien. I summon my servant, but he does not answer, though I beg him with my own mouth. My breath is offensive to my wife; I am loathsome to my own brothers. Even the little boys scorn me; when I appear, they ridicule me. All my intimate friends detest me; those I love have turned against me. I am nothing but skin and bones; I have escaped with only the skin of my teeth. Have pity on me, my friends, have pity, for the hand of God has struck me. Why do you pursue me as God does? Will you never get enough of my flesh?" (Job 19:13-20).

I knew that my large open wound and my colostomy looked and smelled disgusting! At times, I could not stomach the sight and smell of them. Still, no matter how I looked, or how my wound smelled, I was never alone. God supplied every single person who was part of His plan to care for me, and each one willingly answered God's call to serve. I was never, ever alone!

God was not uncaring towards Job! God cares deeply about all our concerns, big or small. However, at this time in Job's life, I think God was more worried about Job's character, and less about how Job felt or his physical state. God allowed all the horrible pain and suffering Job faced, knowing that his testing would prove Job's own personal convictions were honest, and he was not just faithful because it was of some benefit to him. Job proved once more that he was blameless in his love and faithfulness towards God.

When I think about Dr. Touloukian and the fact that he left my long and deep surgical wound open, I can better understand this concept. The surgeon really did care that my huge open wound was difficult to manage and very painful. Surely, he was not so insensitive that he didn't care how ugly I felt, or how infection oozed continually from fistulas inside my body. I know for a fact that my surgeon was very sympathetic regarding all the horrible problems I faced because the wound was left open.

Dr. Touloukian cared more about the fact that I would have died from massive infection if he had sutured the wound shut! There would have been no way for the infection to escape, and no possibility of the wound healing. However, because the surgeon did not suture the wound, but left it open to heal from the inside out, it assured that the abdominal tissues had the very best possible chance to heal completely without being compromised by massive infection. So, as far as the surgeon was concerned, if it meant I would have to hurt, and I might cry because of the pain, so be it. He made a choice to do what he felt was best for me. He was confident I would be successful in living with the challenges of the open wound, that I'd have complete healing of the wound, and that I would LIVE!

Likewise, God really did care about Job's uncomfortable situation, but He cared even more about the man Job was becoming – He cared more about Job's character. If it meant that Job would continue to suffer, so be it. In the end, Job became the man God intended him to be – upright and blameless. He would LIVE and be blessed with so much more than he ever dreamed possible.

Chapter 19

Horizon of Hope (March 2006, Home)

At my first post-op visit, Dr. Touloukian told me there was a possibility that I could have my colostomy reversed in three to six months. This was the second time I was told the reversal was a possibility, and I was more than thrilled to hear the news. That was a huge incentive for me to get better.

I still had so much trouble with my colostomy, and it leaked constantly. I often referred to my lower abdomen as the "Butternut Bread" belly, because I had a huge crater in the middle of my abdomen that was deep and jagged all along the edges on both sides of the wound. The skin around the stoma was not flat either, compliments of my "Butternut Bread" belly. The colostomy was so close to the wound that it was next to impossible to get the colostomy appliances to hold.

My "Butternut Bread" belly made life with a colostomy miserable! It cost me a small fortune to buy all the additional supplies I needed, and there was the issue of clothing. I was limited to stretch pants or sweats, because the colostomy was directly in line with my waist band, so everything I wore put pressure on the stoma and restricted the flow. When my bag filled up, the huge bulge was very evident. I remember how I worried when I was in a department store that people might think I was stealing and hiding merchandise under my shirt because of how the bag pooched out.

I was extremely self-conscious and hated how I looked. I had no intention of liking that colostomy, or even thinking about its being permanent. I would deal with it for now, but I was determined to have the colostomy reversed just as soon as Dr. Touloukian allowed it. I did not know how God would accomplish it, but I knew He would give me a miracle so I would no longer need the colostomy. I prayed for God to hear my prayers. I saw firsthand how the power of prayer can move the heart of God, and I wanted to be free of the colostomy in the worst way.

"How great is God – beyond our understanding! The number of his years is past finding out. He draws up the drops of water, which distill as rain to the streams; the clouds pour down their moisture and abundant showers fall on mankind. Who can understand how he spreads out the clouds, how he thunders from his pavilion? See how he scatters his lightning about him, bathing the depths of the sea. This is the way he governs the nations and provides food in abundance" (Job 36:26-31).

God is Omniscient, Magnificent, and Omnipotent! Surely, He would honor my prayer. I trusted that my God would hear me and answer, but did I listen, or was I only willing to hear a YES to my request?

I wonder what state of mind I was in when I longed for the colostomy reversal. God provided a way for me to have a new lease on life and time with my family, yet I was not satisfied with His provisions. Perhaps, I needed to repent for my lack of gratitude for God's provision and blessing.

Chapter 20

The Well Runs Dry (April 2006, Home)

As might be imagined, our finances were a constant concern. There were mounting medical bills that we knew we might never be able to pay, and we came close to losing our home many times. We prayed, we cried, and we stressed! There were times I just watched my world unravel before my eyes, and I could not control my life or finances any longer.

It was time to let go, and give it all to God. I had no idea how we were going to make it, but God did. I was tired – so tired of running the show. Every time I sat down to do bills, the tears welled up in my eyes. I moved money from one account to another just praying it would cover us one more month. We sold, cancelled, refinanced, or consolidated all we could. The well was dry, and I was out of ideas. Our house was on the market, but we hadn't had a single offer.

Job was so wise, and he knew better than to try to run the show. Oh, he was not happy with how the situation was unfolding, but he knew that he needed to give his monstrous problem to God. He must have felt like he'd been to hell and back, and I imagine the peace and comfort he must have felt in turning it all over to God. Hanging on to the immense pain, frustration and anxiety is more than anyone can endure.

I welcomed the relief I felt as I learned to let go – really let go and let God. Let me say, it wasn't easy! I'm a control freak; I'm not proud of it, but it's the truth. I am also a perfectionist, and that is partly the cause of my control issues. I knew God did not cause my medical problems, but He did allow it. He's been teaching me a host of lessons, but two that He has taught me is that I am selfish and that I have a lot of pride. In spite of my hubris, God continued to work in me. I don't know it all, and I can't do everything, no matter how hard I try.

I'd been praying and asking God to help us with our finances, but I let my pride and selfishness get in the way of His plan. There were people who could have helped us, but I declined their offer, thinking we could handle it. I didn't want to trouble anyone, knowing God would help us. Oh, how blind I was. When I didn't see any changes in our situation, and circumstances seemed to be getting even more critical, I cried out to God.

"God, what's going on? You promised You would supply all our needs and You have. We have food and shelter, and I praise You for all our blessings! I am sorry I question You so much, but I don't understand. These hospital bills just keep climbing, and they want their money. We don't have it, and I'm not sure how long the hospital will continue to help me without payment. Please show me what to do." As soon as I said those words, "Show me what to do," I felt the most sickening feeling in the pit of my stomach.

God spoke to me. "I AM. I am sufficient!"

I still tried to take control! I begged God for help, gave Him my problems, and then I grabbed them back when my problems weren't getting "fixed" as quickly as I'd like. I was so ashamed, because we saw firsthand how God provided for us when it seemed impossible. God is enough, and there's no doubt about that!

Many times our monthly bills exceeded our funds in the checking account by hundreds of dollars, yet we were able to pay every bill for the month. It made no sense and was not humanly possible, but God did it! I still can't explain it, but I know God provided a miracle, so why did I doubt Him now? I felt horrible, and it seemed there were no words to express how sorrowful I was. I could barely get the words out to beg for His forgiveness; I was broken. I must have hurt Jesus in the very worst way, but perhaps not. Jesus understands.

As I sobbed, I felt an overwhelming sense of love and forgiveness come over me. He forgave me, but He wasn't finished teaching me. He revealed another sin I had not realized. He brought special people into my life to fulfill part of His plan for me and my family. Those special people who came to us wanting to help us were being cheated of a blessing. I rejected their offer to help, and they were not allowed to use their gifts and talents as God intended.

My pride became a stumbling block as I denied them the opportunity to be a blessing! Never, in a million years, would I purposely deny someone of being a blessing, but I did, because I didn't want to be a burden. What had I done? The truth: I really did need them, and I screwed up God's plan royally! Now what? I was afraid to ask.

I hung onto my job for a brief time after I got sick, because I had accumulated quite a bit of sick time, vacation, and holidays, but eventually my job ended, and so did the insurance. I found myself reflecting on the three employers I had worked for over the past twenty-eight years, and I realized God's marvelous provisions.

My first job was with Drs. Childress, Weimer, and Weigel, O.D.'s. I started working for the doctors when I was a junior in high school, and worked there until 1986. Those eight years went by very quickly, and I felt as if I'd grown up with those people. The doctors were very good to me, and it was a tremendous place to work. I really enjoyed working with the patients, too. We were a small company, and we took great pride in how we valued and cared for our patients. I learned a lot about customer service, about hard work, and about good Christian relationships.

My parents drilled good work ethics into all thirteen of us children. I didn't mind hard work, and I seemed to perform best when I was challenged, or on a time crunch. As much as I appreciated my job, I really wanted to be a mommy. I quit working for the optometrists when my daughter, Megan, was born and, to my delight, they hired my mother to fill my position. I was thrilled that she would be working in a place where the employers cared so much for their employees and their patients. God's timing, as usual, was perfect. Years later when I became sick, the staff proved to be a source of prayer and encouragement. I thanked God for those doctors and their continued friendship.

My second employer was the Medical Multi-Specialty Clinic. I went back to work when Megan was eight months old and basically walked into the job. I didn't even have an interview; I heard there was an opening; I called, and they asked when I could start. That was God going before me and preparing the way.

How fortunate to have this job that was a perfect fit for me, but that made it even more difficult to leave. I worked at the clinic for thirteen years. There were five family practice doctors and a Physician assistant: Drs. Domingo, McCullough, Alunday, Mungcal, the Rufino's, and Rick Meyers, P.A.C. Dr. Fletcher joined the practice later, but all the doctors were, and are, amazing individuals. I had a very good working relationship with all the doctors, and I grew to cherish them, as well as my co-workers. All the doctors participated in my healthcare; however, Dr. Mary McCullough is my primary care doctor, and she is incredible! I pray for her everyday; in fact, I pray for all of my former employers each day. The clinic staff made important and lasting impressions on me and my family, and I thank God for the gift of that job and for the fantastic friends I was blessed with.

My third job was another gift from God, and my employers, Don Horan and Mark Schabel, exemplified Godly leadership. As I contemplated my resignation from their employment, I praised God for His provision of employment at CAI and the employees who became an extension of my family.

A flood of emotions spun around in my head and in my heart. I pushed myself to go back to work at CAI after several months of being on medical leave. I tried to do my job to the very best of my ability, but I was finally forced to quit in March of 2007 when I could not drag myself into work anymore. Don and Mark were exceedingly patient with me, but it was time for me to go so I could concentrate on getting well!

I sat down at my computer at home and wrote my letter of resignation. Tears streamed down my face. I treasured my job, each employee, and each staff member. We cared deeply about one another; physically, emotionally, and spiritually. They sent me numerous care packages while I was in the hospital and while I recuperated at home. My favorite gift was a bouquet of beautiful construction paper flowers. Each employee and staff member wrote a personal note on one of the flowers, and the tender notes were a sweet reminder of the special bond we had.

I was so emotional and I cried out to God. "What will I do now? How will Larry and I survive without my working? What about all these medical bills? God, You have never failed me, and I will continue to trust in You. I love You so much, God, and I thank

You for allowing me the opportunity to share in these people's lives – their times of great joy and their times of grueling struggles."

I truly desired to honor God in the way I dealt with my illness, and in all the different procedures and surgeries I would still have to endure, because I did not want to be bitter. I was the recipient of many miracles, and I wanted to let others know and see what God did for me.

Still, I had so many questions, and I was so unsettled in my spirit. There was no certainty of the future for me, yet I was excited to see what God would do in all of this. All I could do was trust in God's unfailing love for me and His plan for my life. I worked on my letter of resignation for almost three hours. I'd write a few sentences, quit, and then come back to it. Then I'd write a bit more, quit, and come back again, and when I finished the letter I was drained.

My drive to work the following morning was marked by mascara running down my face. I cried before I even left the house, and as soon as I saw Mark, I just handed him my letter. I couldn't even speak … he couldn't hold back either. We were both in tears.

Of all days, Don did not come in that morning. I wanted to talk to him personally and let him know how much I loved and appreciated him, but that would have to wait for another day.

Mark called a staff meeting and told all the employees I was leaving. I stayed in my office because I did not have the strength physically or emotionally to hold up. As the employees left the meeting, they all filed past my office, greeted me with hugs and kisses, and wished me the very best. I was dying inside; it was much harder than I ever expected. As my friends walked me out to my car, I gave them one last hug and drove away. I left feeling very loved and blessed having had the job, and I was fortunate for having made such incredible friends.

Over and over I have benefitted in some fashion by past employers or co-workers. They have been a significant part of my healing process: emotionally, spiritually and financially. I didn't deserve the astonishing expressions of love and kindness, but I was so appreciative for every gift.

It was a huge blessing when our church, First Baptist Church of Greensburg, hosted a benefit for me and my family and for the Wyatt family to help with our medical expenses. It was a fabulous evening, and there were so many people who came to support both our families. Even more, another church, Sand Creek Baptist, hosted a second benefit for me! That was totally unexpected and very much appreciated! That money came just in the nick of time to save our home from foreclosure. There were other churches in our area that supported us as well, and it seemed the whole community came together on our behalf. Our money problems were far from over, but God intervened and allowed us these marvelous blessings. We praised God before the benefits, and we praise God now. He is forever faithful!

Job continued to plead his case to God. *"If I have put my trust in gold or said to pure gold, 'You are my security,' if I have rejoiced over my great wealth, the fortune my hands had gained, ... then these also would be sins to be judged, for I would have been unfaithful to God on high"* (Job 31:24, 25, 28).

Job was highly revered and very wealthy, but he worked exceedingly hard for all he gained, and he did not make money his idol. Job did not sin in his management of his wealth. He was faithful … and still, Job lost everything!

There are times when I have wished for a windfall of money, but I know how money can destroy a man's life if it becomes his idol. When my family was blessed with two benefits, we used the money to pay down our medical debt and to make house payments, so we would continue to have a roof over our heads. We wanted to be faithful in dealing with the money God provided. Bankruptcy was not an option, and we believe when we incur a debt we are responsible to pay that debt, period! Even after we got caught up on our house payments, we were still fearful of falling into foreclosure. We didn't understand why our home had not sold when it was on the market for so long.

Throughout the years of medical mayhem, Larry and I encountered many unknowns, including our finances. We were in unfamiliar territory, and we had many difficult decisions to make. In all our endeavors, our desire was for God to be glorified and, like Job, we chose to trust God!

Chapter 21

No More Colostomy (May 9, 2006, I.U. Medical Center)

At a follow-up appointment in April of 2006, Dr. Touloukian said he would consider doing the colostomy reversal in May or June if I continued to improve as I had. Yeah, no more colostomy!

Dr. Touloukian wrote an order for the pre-op tests. I had to have a heart catheterization to make sure I did not have any further heart issues, and I needed more lab work and additional X-rays. Then Dr. Touloukian warned me about the surgical risks and cautioned me about the long difficult road to recovery associated with a colostomy reversal. He said the recovery could last anywhere from twelve weeks to six months. When the bowel is reconnected to the rectum, patients experience explosive diarrhea for several weeks or even months, and sometimes up to a year! The diarrhea is very caustic, and it literally creates chemical burns when it makes contact with the skin. He said there were creams to help with the irritation and sores, and he also suggested that I purchase several packages of disposable undergarments.

I assured Dr. Touloukian I was up to the challenge. "Wow, it must be horrific diarrhea! I am not looking forward to that, but I am determined to deal with whatever comes, because I know God will get me through it."

"Okay," Dr. Touloukian said, "it's a go for the surgery, and we'll do the surgery on May 9th."

Praise the Lord! I was elated, and I began counting down the days to my surgery. On May 9, 2006, I arrived at the I.U. Medical Center for my surgery to have the colostomy reversed.

Around 8:00 a.m. the nurses finally allowed my family to come back to the pre-op room so they could pray with me before the surgery. There were about thirty family members packed into that small surgical holding room, and I was completely surrounded by the people I love most – my family. We sang praise and worship songs, and then we prayed. The Spirit of God filled that place, and several were moved to tears; I found myself fighting back tears, too. Dr. Touloukian remarked how impressed he was that my family was so large and so supportive. I agreed!

"At this my heart pounds and leaps from its place. Listen! Listen to the roar of his voice, to the rumbling that comes from his mouth. He unleashes his lightning beneath the whole heaven and sends it to the ends of the earth. After that comes the sound of his roar; he thunders with his majestic voice. When his voice resounds, he holds nothing back" (Job 37:1-4).

I was ready for God to do His miracle, and I believed I would come through with flying colors. Soon I would be on my way to a complete recovery.

Chapter 22

Something's Not Right (May 2006, I.U. Medical Center)

Dr. Touloukian came to the surgery waiting area to let the family know that I made it through: however; it was not an easy surgery. He had a very difficult time dealing with all the adhesions again, and he commented that I'd grown a significant amount of new adhesions since the last surgery. He was satisfied with the procedure and did not anticipate any complications, but he planned on keeping me for several days to make sure everything was working as it should before he let me go home. Praise the Lord; He brought me through another surgery.

The first day after surgery wasn't too bad, as I was still heavily sedated. I was not allowed to get up to the bathroom, so I was forced to use a bed pan, and that was a mess.

Dr. Touloukian was right; I had absolutely NO warning prior to a bowel movement or diarrhea, so I had several accidents. Today was not a very good day, but surely tomorrow would be better.

Oh, my goodness! Ouch! Talk about caustic! The diarrhea was killing me! The anesthesia had completely worn off by now, and I was feeling the full fledged effects of the very painful effluent! The nurses tried to get me up to a potty chair, but every time I started to get up, it was already too late. How could this happen?

The nurse finally decided it was time for a diaper. Here we go – stripped of all dignity, I was one big mess; physically and emotionally. It was extremely embarrassing to have to wear diapers again! I was in a tremendous amount of pain, and I could not understand why I was not getting more relief as I headed into the third day post-surgery. Dr. Touloukian was not overly concerned, and he felt the next day would be a turning point for me. He was troubled, however, that I would not be able to handle the large volume of diarrhea I was having, and he admitted it was quite a bit more than even he expected.

My bottom was speckled with burns due to the caustic diarrhea; still, I was not willing to give up. I was determined to get past this and move on with my life. I was nauseated, and I started vomiting again – I couldn't understand why.

About mid-afternoon I noticed a brown spot, about the size of a quarter, of a wet substance leaking through my bandages on my abdomen. I had a sinking feeling in my gut that this was a very bad situation, and I uttered a short prayer before I hit the call light. "Please, God, not again. Let this be anything but stool." I showed the nurse what I discovered, and she had a puzzled look on her face. She did not say what she thought it might be, but she said she needed to check something and she'd be right back. Within five minutes there was a whole team of surgeons taking down my bandages and checking out the wound. Their faces told the story. Unfortunately, that brown substance was stool. Not again! My bowel was leaking, and I was so disappointed and hurting. Dr. Touloukian talked to Larry and me and said he had no choice but to go back to the operating room to fix the leak. Our worst nightmare was coming true. I thought the surgery would be scheduled for the following day, but to my surprise, I would be in the operating room within the hour.

Nurses came and went, and I was poked and prodded from every direction.

As one of the nurses came rushing in, I saw the long line of tubing she carried. Oh no, not an NG tube! I had been repeatedly tortured with having nasal gastric tubes. I panicked!

"No, you can't do that! You will not touch me with that! Please, you can put that in while I'm in surgery! There is no need to torture me when I'm going to surgery any time now!" The nurse was insistent that it must be done immediately; I was agitated and I told her I wanted to see Dr. Touloukian right now! No one was going to touch me until I talked to him!

After a few moments of hesitation, the nurse finally paged the surgeon, and he came fairly quickly. I think he thought there was another emergency, but I didn't care. This WAS an emergency to me! Dr. Touloukian explained to me that he was concerned about the fact that I'd already started vomiting, and he wanted to make sure he was able to get the tube in before there was any swelling or other problem. He could see I was not in any shape to argue this case, but he also did not want to traumatize me any further. Reluctantly, he did agree to wait until I was in surgery before the tube was inserted.

"Thank You, Jesus!" That was a huge answered prayer.

Larry made calls to the family, and I could feel my anxiety level standing at an all time high. The tension was terrible, and I knew this was bad, but I avoided asking the tough questions because I did not want all the gory details, and I wanted to be able to be as positive as possible going into the surgery. Larry called the church, the prayer chain started, and in the course of the conversation with the surgeon, I heard Larry mention something about the fact that I might not make it!

When did Dr. Touloukian say that? Had I just blocked it out? I wasn't scared about the possibility of dying, but I was extremely nervous about the possibility of living through the surgery and then being messed up so badly that I would end up in a nursing home, so I began to pray. The locks on the bed clanked down, and I was wheeled out of my room at breakneck speed.

Larry caught Megan between classes, so she was able to make it back to the hospital within fifteen minutes. Sam, on the other hand, could not make it. I hated that he was so far away, and he was already afraid something terrible would happen. He was forced to wait at school, a couple of hours away, to hear how I did in surgery. I know the waiting was devastating.

In the operating room, I saw the familiar super bright light just above my head. It was very cold, and I began to shiver and my teeth chattered. Also, my nerves were beginning to get the best of me. Soon a nurse came with those wonderful heated blankets, and what a blessing that was! The anesthesiologist said the surgeon would be in any moment if I had any questions, but if I didn't have any questions he would go ahead and sedate me. That was a no brainer; I just wanted this to be over!

After the surgery, Dr. Touloukian told Larry and the family that between the times of my surgery two days earlier and today, a significant amount of new adhesions formed again! He was amazed at the rate in which my body continued to produce adhesions. He tried feverishly to seal the leak, but he did not know if it was completely sealed. Also, Dr. Touloukian had to leave the wound open again. There was a host of infection, and the wound needed to heal from the inside out.

I was amazed that the wound was just as large as the first surgery, and I could not believe I was starting all over again trying to get it healed. God brought me through so much, but how much more could I stand? It was so painful when I shifted in bed – especially when I tried to turn on my side for the nurse to clean me up or to change my diaper. I lost all sense of modesty, and there were so many doctors and nurses constantly looking at my battered torso, it was pathetic. I'd just get covered up and someone else would need to have a look. I tried to smile and be cordial, but I was really frustrated, and I desperately needed some privacy.

I also struggled with how all the scars, tubes, and bags might be affecting Larry. He never complained or mentioned them to me, but I prayed constantly that God would give me the strength to face what I would look like when the doctors finished with me. I honestly felt like Frankenstein's monster!

I asked Dr. Touloukian if there was any chance that I could have cosmetic surgery to correct all the ugly scars, but he said absolutely nothing could be done. Not only had I formed a massive network of adhesions on the inside, but I also formed keloid scars on the outside. My surgical scars looked like big wide sections of dried snake skin that had been shed. The surgeon explained that trying to remove the scars would only make matters worse.

I don't know how he could possibly know that it would make it any worse, because I was feeling about as ugly as a person could. Believe it or not, it was comforting to me to be covered with bandages. I didn't have to see how bad I looked, and neither did Larry. I had some really bad self-image issues that needed to be addressed, and I wanted to talk to Larry in the worst way. Unfortunately, this was not the time; also, I wondered how critical my health issues really were. Were the doctors keeping problems from me so I would not get so depressed? I asked Dr. Touloukian if he thought the bowel was sealed this time. "There were too many adhesions to get a good look. It will just be a waiting game." I could tell he was bothered by the question, because he didn't have the answer I wanted, and it was hard for him to see my reaction. He really did care.

The waiting is something we came to expect and dread, but I knew better than to ask how long I would be staying in the hospital, so we just prayed and waited. I received calls and cards from hundreds of people, and people from all over the United States prayed for me. I don't know how they all knew about me, but I was sure thankful for every single prayer. My cell phone rang off the hook and so did Larry's; our cell phone bill that month was over $500.00!

The diarrhea got worse, and the nurses didn't even bother to use a bed pan anymore. They just waited until I soiled the diapers, and then they cleaned me up. My skin was so broken down that I had jagged patches of infection with snotty green drainage. The nurses were really good about coming right away to clean me up, because they wanted to stay on top of the infection. The smell reeked! The nurses said it was partly from the diarrhea, but mostly caused by the fetid infection. Of course, I could not help it, but this just compounded the terrible self-esteem issues I experienced. I was embarrassed and I couldn't tolerate the smell either, and it made me feel dirty and disgusting!

Meg has a very keen sense of smell. When she lost much of her hearing several years prior, she developed a much stronger sense of smell. She would gag and hold her breath when she came into my room, but the nurses would not allow us to use the room deodorizer that Megan brought in. The only spray we were allowed to use was the hospital's version of a deodorizer, and it had no smell at all! It was ridiculous! So, when the nurses left the room, Meg would spray a little of her cologne she had in her purse, but it didn't help much.

I didn't know how we were going to keep the infection under control as long as the diarrhea occurred so often, and I was very concerned about how I would manage all this when I got home, too. Who would stay with me day and night to change the diapers? I was so embarrassed, and I wouldn't want my worst enemy to have to deal with this.

"Terrors overwhelm me; my dignity is driven away as by the wind, my safety vanishes like a cloud. And now my life ebbs away; days of suffering grip me. Night pierces my bones; my gnawing pains never rest" (Job 30:15-17).

Job was beaten down, he was in trouble, and he believed his time was short. Because he suffered so fiercely, Job welcomed death, and I understood Job's position. I feared the thought of the next dressing change, the diaper changes, the NG tubes, and all the other tortures that were coming. I could not fathom how I would survive the constant battery of procedures.

Still, I did not fully comprehend the powerful spirit God placed within me. He made the unbearable bearable, and He allowed me to withstand what I thought would consume me. He protected me and sheltered me in the fiercest of storms, just as He protected Job. I wished I could control my emotions a little better, but as I was in the midst of a terrible storm, it didn't matter. I just did what I had to do to make it through. I tried to be so strong for the children, but I feared I had failed them miserably. Then, I remembered something I'd heard a minister say once about how we look at our adversities.

"Do we believe that God is picking on us and find ourselves disappointed in how our life is unfolding, or do we believe that God has picked us out?"

Sometimes I feel that I have been "picked on" instead of being "picked out," and I believe that Job felt that way at times as well. What we both needed to be thinking instead was that God chose us! He did not pick on us. We have grown to a point in our faith that we have become worthy of God's increased investment in us and He's ready to take us to another level. He is challenging us and preparing us for a new season in our life. We will see blessings and incredible miracles happen when we move forward with God, and with the mindset that we have been chosen for His special service. On the pathway of life, others can be fences or bridges. The difference is determined by the steps we take. We CAN make a difference in the world for Christ.

God continually brings me through, and I can only pray that I have not disappointed Him. I want Him to be honored and glorified, and as long as He keeps bringing me back, I'll keep giving my best for Him.

Thank You, Jesus, for picking me out for Your Kingdom's work.

Chapter 23

How Much More Can One Person Take, Lord?
(May 19, 2006, I.U. Medical Center)

In the meanwhile, Larry's mother, Lois, who was very ill from complications with her diabetes, took a turn for the worse. Larry received word that she was dying, and she was taken to a Hospice facility in Columbus, Indiana, almost an hour away from my hospital. The whole family was alerted and made their way to the Hospice facility. Larry wrestled over leaving me, but I finally convinced him to go be with his mom because I did not want him to have any regrets.

Larry and the children went to see Lois, but no one knew just how long it might be before she would pass. My family came to see me early in the day, and then headed over to see Lois in the afternoon. This made for very long and extremely stressful days, so Larry's nerves were raw and he was exhausted! It was only by the grace of God that he held up through all of this. I knew Larry wanted to be with his mom, but he was so worried about me. I kept praying for Larry, and I asked God to give him an abundance of strength and endurance; I love him so much, and I was extremely worried about him. He acquired huge dark circles under his eyes, and his face was long and drawn. Sam, Megan, and I looked the same way; we were all a pitiful mess. Although Larry and the children saw Lois as much as they could, they spent the majority of their time with me, and I was thankful for that.

I was also thankful that Larry had other siblings to be with his mom. His sisters carried the brunt of the support, and they did not want to leave their mother's side, but they felt sympathy for me, too. Larry's sisters were where they needed to be, and I understood this. I felt so sorry for all Larry, his dad and his siblings were going through, but I could not help the situation.

I struggled, too, because I wanted so much to see Lois before she died. I wanted to see her and to tell her … one last time that I loved her, but that just was not going to happen.

Finally, a servant told Job that his sons and daughters were all killed when a wind swept up and struck the four corners of the house. The home collapsed on them, and in the blink of an eye, Job lost all that he worked for – his possessions and his family; still, he retained his soul.

I loved Larry's mom, and as sorry as I was that I could not be with her, I was so thankful that she belonged to Jesus. Because she was a Christian, it was better that we let her go … heaven frees us from all pain.

I wasn't sure where I would be in the next few days myself. Maybe I would join her in heaven because I had no assurance one way or the other, except that God kept bringing me back. I wished I understood the most important concerns I should be experiencing. Was it all about my family members who didn't know Jesus, or was it something more? What was my specific purpose? Why was I still here?

I do know that God commissions each of us to GO and spread the Good News. I must share the Gospel of Jesus Christ with everyone I can. As one very wise person said, "I want to tell the whole world about Jesus, and I'll use words if necessary."

Chapter 24

It Happened Again (May 2006, I.U. Medical Center)

Two days after the surgery I was again in a panic! Oh, my goodness! It happened again! A thick, dark drainage seeped through my bandages. This was very bad, and I knew the extreme risk of another surgery. For the first time in a long while, I was really, really scared! I was not afraid to die; I was afraid of the pain, and I was scared how I might survive with horrible complications and, this time, I really might end up in a nursing home. That thought had terrified me!

"Okay, God, I know You said You would give me no more than I can bear, but this is over the top! I'm a mess here, and I need help right now! Please fix this. I am begging You. Please don't let me end up in a nursing home!" I cried out for God's mercy. Strangely, Dr. Touloukian came in to see what was going on, and he immediately ordered the nurse to get a medication.

Then Dr. Touloukian said, "Deborah, we're going back to surgery." His eyes were fixed on mine as he talked. "Hang in there. I'll do everything I can."

I must have looked like a caged animal, because the surgeon rubbed my arm and just kept speaking very slowly and softly to me until the nurse came with the medication he ordered. As soon as I received the medication in my IV, I was out. Fortunately, my family was at the hospital when the decision was made to go back to surgery. It all happened so fast, and before I knew it, I was once again whisked into the operating room for the third time in less than two weeks!

Again, I didn't understand why God kept me alive; what was my "real" purpose and what could I do for Him in this condition? Yet, by the grace of God and prayers from all over the United States, I made it through surgery, again! I honestly do not remember much of anything about either the preparation for the surgery or what happened afterward. Thankfully, I was heavily sedated, but my mind ran away from me. I was a "train wreck," but God wasn't finished with me.

Later, when I told visitors about the ordeal, they were utterly amazed that I was still alive and, quite frankly, so was I. It was a miracle, an absolute miracle that I survived this, because of the extent of my surgeries and the infection that ravaged my body. I give God all the praise and honor for what He did in me. I certainly appreciated Dr. Touloukian, and I believe even he recognized that a higher power was responsible for my still being alive.

I thought about how Job endured so much and still lived. Job had incredible strength and faith. We all bleed and we all fall. Job often prayed for death because of his terrible physical condition and loss. What specific purpose was there for Job to live? God commanded Satan that he could do whatever he wanted to Job, but not take his life. God had a plan to bring Job out of his misery. So I wondered, what was the plan? Unfortunately, Job didn't know the plan either, and that made his plight all the worse. All Job had was his faith – and hope against all hope – that his God would deliver him and restore his good name.

I believe God extended His hand to Job to guard his every step should he stumble. God allowed Satan to inflict pain in Job's life, but Job's life would be spared just as God commanded. God didn't turn His back on Job; He was there in every circumstance, and He never left him. That's how much God cares about each one of us. It is God's deep love for me: His endless, unconditional love that has sustained me in all of my calamities, and I am sure it is what sustained Job, too.

A few days after the third surgical attempt to repair my bowel leak, Larry's mom passed away. Family, friends, and our church were there to support Larry and the children more than ever. The family was exhausted, and they struggled with the death, as well as my situation. I was devastated, too, and I prayed that Lois would live long enough for me to be released from the hospital, and that I would be able to see her one last time, but God did not grant my prayer. He did grant Larry's Mother the gift of a swift reunion with

Him in heaven. I wondered why her death came in the midst of all that we were already dealing with. Could it get any worse?

"Jesus, I just don't get it! What is the problem? These are supposed to be the very best surgeons. Let them find the leak and fix it for good! What are You trying to teach me? I'm obviously NOT getting it! Did I do something wrong? If I'm being punished for something I've done, show me what it is! I'm sorry, truly sorry if I have done something against You or anyone. Please forgive me. Please, Jesus – I don't want anything to stand between us. I love You, Lord! I feel like a cat losing its nine lives. How much more can my body take, and when will my number be up? I survived all these other surgeries, and it's getting harder and harder to bounce back. I feel like it's all been a big tease. I make it through and then, boom! – there's another problem. I can't take it anymore! Rescue me, Jesus. Please heal me or just let me die! Heal my body right now, right here! Whatever happens God, I will love You and I will still praise You, but I need answers and I need them NOW!" I didn't mince words with Jesus.

I was extremely weak and beyond tired, but I was feisty! Because my emotions were running at an all-time high, all I knew to do was to pour my heart out to God, because He was the only One who could help me and the only One who truly understood. One of the blessings that came from my trials and tribulations is my incredible relationship with Jesus. I need Him so much, and I talk to Him as if He is my best friend just standing right here in front of me. He is so real to me.

Jesus loves that I tell Him how I'm feeling. I have nothing to hide, and couldn't even if I wanted to; He understands my frustration. He doesn't strike me with a lightning bolt when I question Him, although He could. He listens, He knows my desperation, He knows how badly I want to be healed, and He knows whatever the outcome, I will praise Him.

Since God is working His plan, I will just roll with the punches. In the end, the result will be just as it is meant to be. He is in control, and I am NOT. I said what I needed to say, and I am okay with whatever God will do in me or through me from this moment on. I am at peace with it – ALL of it.

It became apparent to family, friends, and others that God was the sole reason I was still here. Dr. Touloukian was only an instrument – an excellent one, I might add. However, he did not have the control. God used him to accomplish His will in my life, and as all the surgeries began to unfold, and I survived each one, I believe Dr. Touloukian and the residents witnessed many miracles and the power of God.

Sam and Megan were puzzled. "Mom, you talk about all your surgeries like it's no big deal! You don't get angry or even curse; you're not mad at God, you don't get mad at the doctors, and you don't even cry. Do you know how sick you are and how many times you could have died?"

Yes, I certainly did. As horrible as it was to endure, I continued to survive. God granted me many miracles which no one could dispute, and through my weakness and pain, God was glorified! People understood that mere mortal men (no matter how proficient the surgeons might be) could not be responsible for my still being alive.

Meg was frustrated and infuriated! She wanted to pull me up off that bed and take me to another hospital right then. She has always been very protective of me, and I know her heart was to get me to someone, anyone, who would fix this. Her face turned fiery red, and she could barely get her words out. Sam just sat with his face in his hands. He didn't say a word, and he could barely look at me as he struggled so hard to hold it all together. He's very tender-hearted, and he could not stand to see me suffer. I told Sam and Megan they needed to let go of their pain and frustration. I would recover, but the load of worry was just too much for them. I reasoned with them: "It is only by the grace of God and His great compassion towards me that I have survived to this point. God has been with me every step of the way, and He has sustained me. I am not afraid, and I am at peace; total peace. I know you love me, but you do not have to worry about me. God is protecting me, and He still has a purpose for me here on earth. If I could have shielded you two from any of this I would have. Please try to understand. This is a journey that I have to take, and I can't make it without God. I need you, too. You have to be strong." They didn't say a word as they took it all in.

A heavy cloud hung over my room that day, and I hated that my children were hurting so much. I believe they thought I was in some kind of denial, because I wasn't completely falling apart or angry all the time. I realized when I told people how I was doing, or what was going on at the time, I downplayed the situation, and it sounded as though my condition was not nearly as serious as it was. I purposely left out many gory details and incidents that complicated my situation, because it didn't really benefit anyone to know those circumstances – least of all me.

Believe me, it was horrific, and no one knew that better than I! I just chose to focus on and talk about the positive rather than the cruel and insane realities I often faced. "What's happened is past and I can't wallow in self-pity. I make a choice every day, sometimes every minute, to be joyful and to cherish each moment, each breath I have." I wanted my children to understand how important it was for me to focus on Jesus. I needed every ounce of energy I had to survive, and the only way I could accomplish that was to keep my eyes on Jesus.

I experienced so many miracles of coming through the surgeries time and time again that I had, quite literally, come to expect the miracles, and I think most of my family did as well. We were all desensitized to the fact that I could have and, according to the surgeon, should have, died more than once! We saw the awesome power of God at work in my body and spirit! How could we not trust Him? The surgeons may have been holding the scalpel, but God did the cutting!

"Yes, but aren't you sad to think that if you die, Sam and I won't have a mom? We still need you and Dad needs you!" Meg was still troubled by what she thought was my lackadaisical attitude, and perhaps she was, unknowingly, being selfish. On one hand Meg was furious with me, and on the other hand she was glad I wasn't falling apart at the seams. She wanted to be so grown up and purposeful. After all, she is one strong-willed and independent young woman. Still, I could see she was just about to explode.

"Yes, I know exactly how hard it is on both of you and on your dad. I love you more than you can ever imagine. Don't you ever question that! I did not ask for this, and I would not have chosen to put any of us through what we have endured, but the fact is, it happened and we have to deal with it. I'm sorry it has been so hard on you, especially with you two in school and not able to be here at the hospital with me as much as you want. You have no idea what goes on when you are not here. You don't see me when I'm all alone late at night and desperate for comfort. You don't know how I lean so heavily on God every minute, and sometimes every second, of the day just to survive. I have cried many tears, but I don't want my children to see their mother crying and in pain. I know you want to help me, and your dad is doing everything he can do, too, but all any of us can really do is pray and accept that God will take care of me!

The only way I know to cope is to trust God completely. If I go into a surgery with a defeated and fearful attitude, I may not make it. This is my journey, and I have to find a way to deal with this. I've learned that I just have to lay the journey in Jesus' lap, and I've let go of as much as I possibly can. God granted me a glimpse of heaven, and I am not afraid. My family's security is what I struggle with the most, and I worry about you constantly! I wish I could promise you that I'll always be here for you, but I can't. All I can say is I'm sorry, and I love you more than words can express!" That was one of the most difficult discussions I have ever had with my children. After a few moments of silence, Meg came and threw herself at me with the biggest hug and kisses ever! Sam was right behind her. I think we used an entire box of Kleenex, but God is good; so … good!

Months later as Meg and I were talking, she told me I was the strongest woman she had ever known, and she was so proud of me. That made me so happy and even now, just as I recall that moment; tears stream down my face. What did I ever do to deserve such wonderful children and such a loving husband? Thank You, Jesus!

Chapter 25

I Just Don't Understand
(End of May 2006, I.U. Medical Center)

Dr. Touloukian cautioned us not to get our hopes up as I headed into day five following the latest surgery without any sign of trouble. Praise the Lord, no signs of trouble, but the surgeon was not entirely convinced the leak was sealed. Again, we had to be patient. Larry and I discussed all the bills coming in. Everyday the mailbox ballooned with new bills. Larry paid the house payment and utility bills, but the medical bills had him overwhelmed. He stacked all the medical bills in a box so I could go through them and determine what could be paid. I have lots of experience in medical insurance billing. I knew better than to pay a medical bill without making sure the insurance carrier has actually processed and paid the claim. Correct adjustments and write-offs also had to be verified. Just because a claim was denied, that did not mean we owed it. I wanted to make sure we were only paying what was our obligation. If we owed it, it would be paid. I didn't know how or when, but we would make arrangements to pay our medical debts and do our best to stick to that promise.

I seemed to be doing a little better, so Larry and I decided this was a good time for him to go back to work. Larry had used up almost all of his family leave time, and we could not afford for him to be off work without pay any longer. I also thought some time away from the hospital would do him a world of good. He was not so easily convinced until I told him we could call each other several times a day so he would know what was going on. I also reminded him that he did not have to worry about my being alone. There were lots of family members and friends who came everyday to see me. I would be just fine. He was not happy about the decision to go back to work, but he knew it was what he needed to do. With a very heavy heart, he returned to work that very day and headed out on his run to Kansas City, Kansas.

Secretly I wanted him to stay, but we really needed the money, and he needed some time away from all the stress. He'd practically been living at the hospital, and with all the extra burden of his mom's illness and death, it was just too much. I couldn't imagine what I would do if something happened to him, and I prayed his work would be a welcome distraction and bring him some relief.

Larry hadn't even been gone a full day when I started feeling worse, and I knew something was wrong. I'm not a doctor, but I've learned to read my body, and I knew my bowel was leaking again. The raging fever was back, and I noticed a very pungent odor came from my wound. The wound, red and hot, indicated infection. Most people would die from the infection, let alone all the other complications, and I had a fleeting thought that I might have to have the colostomy put back in if the leak could not be sealed. If that was the case, I would be okay with it, and I would praise God no matter what the outcome would be.

Dr. Touloukian was called in, and he confirmed that my bowel was leaking again. He asked me where Larry was, and I told him he should be in Kansas City, Kansas, by now. I offered to call Larry and have him come back, but the surgeon insisted on speaking to Larry himself. Dr. Touloukian said he would gather his team, and they would be back in a few minutes to talk with me.

He must have been just outside of my room when he made the call to Larry, because I could hear him as he relayed the terrible news. I spiked a temperature and there was another leak. Dr. Touloukian needed to operate within the hour, and he wanted to know how soon Larry could make it back to the hospital.

"What? Another leak? Can she survive another surgery so soon? Be honest with me – is she going to die?" Larry was completely caught off guard and must have been beside himself as he contemplated the seriousness of my condition. Dr. Touloukian told Larry that the surgery was extremely risky, and he didn't know if I would pull through this time. He would do everything he could, but there was so much working against me that he wanted Larry to be prepared for the worst, and he needed Larry to get here as soon as possible. Poor Larry! He could not catch a break! He was terrified that I would die before he got back, and he would never be able to forgive himself for not being there. He asked himself all kinds of questions. "Why did I agree to go back to work so soon? I was afraid this would happen and now it has!"

Larry told Dr. Touloukian that he would turn around and be at the Medical Center just as soon as he could, but it would be at least ten hours before he could get back to the hospital. He asked Dr. Touloukian to please wait for Megan. There was no way Sam could come back, and he would be devastated! Larry called Megan and Sam to let them know what was going on, and then he called family members to make sure someone would be with Megan as she waited in the surgical waiting room.

Later, Larry told me that the moment he made his last call, he began feeling sick to his stomach. He thought he might vomit or even pass out. For a moment, Larry was literally frozen with fear, and all he could do was drive and pray. For the next ten hours, he prayed and begged God to let me live. At times, he cried so hard he could barely see the road.

The hospital has an impressive teaching program. However, it was exasperating at times having to reiterate my medical history and current symptoms so the residents could learn and discover how to treat patients. A surgeon and his team of four or five residents work together on a six month rotation in each of the different fields of study. I must say, my surgical team, with Dr. Touloukian at the helm, was excellent! God assembled this very special team just to care for me, and I firmly believe that! Six years ago, I knew the first and last names of each resident, but my memory has regressed to the point that I can't remember a single name now. That saddens me because they were such wonderful men and women, and I was privileged to know a little about each of them personally, as well as professionally.

At first my doctors' visits were strictly professional, but eventually the residents became more relaxed, and I saw a personal side of each of them that was unique. There were a couple of residents who loved to joke, and they always made me laugh. Two of the residents were very sensitive. When I got bad news they would reach out to hold my hand, or lag behind as the team left to tell me they would be thinking of me. One resident was especially good at reading me. He was concerned about my emotional and spiritual state and would ask how I was "really" doing or feeling. I was so thankful for the team that God assembled for me.

Dr. Touloukian prepped his team before they all came in to see me. The residents were flanked around him as he shared the news of another leak, and I could see that they were shaken. I'd formed a bond with these residents, and I trusted them with my life! It was very disappointing to them that the leaks kept recurring and that I endured so much pain with all these surgeries. They knew the risks better than I, and they were very concerned.

One by one, I scanned their faces. Their eyes glistened from the excess watering of their eyes. In fact, one of the residents began to tear up so much that she excused herself and left the room. Dr. Touloukian's eyes were very moist and glistening, too, but he held his composure like a trooper. It was a wonderful gift of human compassion that I saw in their faces, and I will never forget that. I know they are supposed to be stoic in their professional duties, but God blessed me in that I was able to see the real men and women in the white coats. They cared – they really cared. What a gift that was for me!

This was the fourth surgery in a matter of just three weeks! I should have been terrified about the operation, but now I was more concerned about Larry than I was about the surgery. I worried driving home in his state of mind might cause him to have a heart attack. I prayed that God would deliver him to me safe and sound.

As I said earlier, I overheard Dr. Touloukian telling Larry that I might not survive the surgery. Any other time that comment would have really troubled me. Instead, I was calm, and I was not the least bit concerned about dying. In fact, I knew that I was most likely NOT going to die. God just kept bringing me back, and in my heart I really expected this to be no different. I had total peace about this surgery, and I knew that God would see me through and I would be all right. For the first time in a long while, I was not even afraid of ending up in a nursing home. This was an epiphany!

God taught me something very important right then – that very moment. I knew in my heart that I had to experience every single event that did transpire. I needed to remember the smallest details of what was happening to me so that I would understand the imperative message God was teaching me. Whatever God wanted me to know, I REALLY wanted to "get it!"

I didn't see Megan before I was taken to surgery, but she was there – bless her heart. She talked back and forth on the phone with Sam and Larry and kept them updated on my progress. She was alone in the surgical waiting room for almost an hour before family members made it back to the hospital. I can't imagine how scared she was, because of all that was going through her mind. She'd gone through such unbelievable pressure, too, and I was worried that she might crumble under the weight of such prolonged stress!

At this, Job got up and tore his robe and shaved his head. Then he fell to the ground in worship and said: "Naked I came from my mother's womb, and naked I will depart. The LORD gave and the LORD has taken away; may the name of the LORD be praised. In all this, Job did not sin by charging God with wrongdoing" (Job 1:20-22).

Worship! Is this man a human being? Who was this Job who could remain faithful under all that he endured? His physical pain was just part of his misery – Job lost ALL his children! He was a man of great faith, and God knew just how much Job could take. Wow! I know I have not suffered nearly as much as Job did. I can identify with some of the physical pain, but Job was tormented with intense emotional pain as well. I don't know what I would have done without the blessing of friends and family. I might be a very bitter person today.

Job longed for comforting words from his friends more than ever, but that was not to be. They disappointed him time and time again, because they believed his problems and suffering were God's punishment for his sin. Job did not have a single earthly friend that truly understood his pain.

"Blessed is the man whom God corrects; so do not despise the discipline of the Almighty" (Job 5:17).

I have been blessed with an additional support system as a member of the Body of Christ. I have church friends who constantly prayed for me and came to my aid. At times, these people pulled me through with their prayers and their own personal faith, when I could not muster the faith I needed on my own. I praise God for their unrelenting spirit and efforts to keep me encouraged and hopeful. They were not willing to let me go or let me give up. When we are saved and become part of the Body of Christ, we are a part of God's family. We are to be like-minded (having the mind of Christ) and we are to love one another as Christ loves us.

Job's friends, who were fellow believers and also part of God's family, were severely lacking in their reflection of God. They said they had come to help Job; to comfort and serve. However, they expressed more interest in judging than serving. Job's friends did nothing that would benefit Job or God. In fact, they made matters much more difficult for Job. Their feeble attempt at helping Job was to "set him straight." They accused, prosecuted, and declared judgment on Job at the same time. They had no intention of letting up until they felt Job fully understood his failing and was ready to pay for his sins. As far as his friends were concerned, their "helping," "comforting," and "serving" had an adverse effect. Job literally begged these men, who were supposed to be friends, for mercy so that he might have a moment's rest.

Job was a servant, and I'm sure he was most comfortable in that role. He proved to be a blessing to his neighbors, brothers, sisters, family, and even strangers over the years. However, now he found himself in a precarious situation. Suddenly, Job was the one desperately in need of help! He was denied the blessing of being served, loved, and comforted; he was denied the most basic acts of kindness; his friends missed out on the rare gift of being a blessing, and Job missed out on the blessing of being the recipient!

When we are willing to serve our brother or sister (in Christ) with a humble and giving heart, we find that we are blessed many times over. Everyone involved is blessed. Jesus came to serve, and He teaches us how to serve, as He is the ultimate example of a humble servant.

God taught me about blessings, and He showed me that I needed to allow others to be a blessing to me. I needed them and they needed me. While it was wonderful to be the receiver, I was far more comfortable being the giver. I believe God also taught me humility in this awkward role reversal. It wasn't as though I didn't appreciate all the comfort and relief I received, but it was unfamiliar territory to me. I was never in a situation where I was dependent on so many people and needed so much help. When I stopped fighting all the attention and requests to help me, I experienced blessings far more than I ever dreamed possible.

One of my best blessings was seeing the joy in the faces of those who were "doing" for me! I thought it was odd that they would be so blessed by helping me, but I experienced the same blessing when I was able to do something special for someone else. God multiplies the blessings over and over. He is so amazing!

I smile just thinking about how much love and support I felt then and still feel today. God is enough! He takes care of my emotional needs, and He provides just as He has promised!

Chapter 26

The Colostomy is Back (June 2006, I.U. Medical Center)

I was alone in my hospital room when the surgeon explained to me the outcome of the surgery. He told me the surgery was a very difficult one because he had limited access to the bowel due to more adhesions; he was left with no choice but to put the colostomy back in, and it would be permanent. Although the possibility of having the colostomy put back had been a fleeting thought prior to the surgery, I was still surprised. My lips quivered and I paused for a moment to pull myself together. "What? How did this happen?"

Dr. Touloukian said he had to put the colostomy back because of the extensive network of adhesions. He attempted to remove some of the adhesions that blocked the area of the leak, but he could not remove enough of them to get a clear view of the leak. With limited access to that area, he doubted that he would be successful in sealing the bowel. The bowels would likely continue to leak, so the colostomy was his only option, and it was my only chance for survival. He also said I would be on complete bowel rest. He explained that I could not eat or drink anything, including chewing gum, for several months – a minimum of three months to start! He did not want the bowel to do any kind of work, and resting the bowel for a significant period of time would allow for the possibility of the bowel healing on its own. If the bowel rest was successful in sealing the bowel leak, I could resume eating and drinking, but I would still never be able to have the colostomy reversed. I would just have to learn to live with it as thousands of other people do.

I dared not talk or I would start crying, so I just listened. Part of me was somewhat relieved that I would not have the painful sores or infection anymore caused by the horrific diarrheas. Still, I wasn't quite sure what to think of all of this, and I was very disturbed.

Dr. Touloukian went on to say that he could not do any type

of additional abdominal surgeries.   There were so many new adhesions that he did not believe I would survive even one more surgery, because the adhesions now joined several organs together, and the bowel had become tied up in that mess. Further surgery would create too great a risk for puncture or injury to what little bowel I had left and to the other organs that were all "glued" together. He asked if I had any questions, and I just shook my head. My lips quivered and my teeth chattered so hard that I was afraid I was going to throw up. I was still foggy enough from the anesthetic that I didn't fully comprehend all he told me, but I understood enough to know that this was very bad news and my life still hung in the balance. All I could do was look at him with fear and pathetic confusion. Dr. Touloukian knew I was on the verge of sobbing, so he reached down and just held my hand for a moment. I think he wanted to cry, too. After a moment or two he let go, gave me a slight smile and said, "I'm sorry. I'm really sorry this all didn't turn out much better for you." Then he turned and walked out.

"Help me, Jesus!" I was all alone, and I needed Larry in the worst way! With the news of all these problems – the leak, the bowel rest, the large open wound, the colostomy, the sores and infection, and the fact that I still had my NG tube, I hit another all-time low! I just wanted to die, but I knew I wouldn't. I pulled the covers over my head and cried.

"God, why is this all happening to me? I have tried to be faithful. I know I am far from perfect and I have much to learn. I am so sorry for the times I've questioned You, and for being so whiney and wimpy, but I do love You, and I do praise You for bringing me through as You have. You must consider me something special to invest so much time and care in me. You won't let me die, so I know You have a purpose for my being here. Am I being tested? Why do some people who hate You seem to be doing just fine, while I continue to struggle so much? Please help me understand. I try to be patient, God, but my patience is running thin, and I can't control my emotions anymore!" I found myself ranting and begging God for answers.

    ... "to those who long for death that does not come, who

search for it more than for hidden treasure," ... *(Job 3:21).* Job lost his home, his good standing in the community, all his livestock, all his earthly possessions; his friends, his children and his health. He was covered from head to toe with horrible boils that itched and oozed with foul-smelling infection. Job lost everything, except his conscience.

I thought about what I have that is of great value to me. I'm not a collector, I'm not sentimental when it comes to objects, and I don't own anything of great monetary value. I appreciate the car and appliances I have because they make my daily living much easier, but God, my family and my health are what I consider to be of greatest value. A few years ago, I felt much differently. I let my work and desires stand in the way of my relationship with Jesus.

It was painful for Job to hear that all his livestock and other earthly possessions were gone. What really caused more pain for Job, however, was the loss of his family and his health. Still, in the process of being stripped completely naked of all he had, Job realized his most precious possession, God, was all he needed. It was in the midst of Job's fieriest trials that God showed Job that his greatest need was God. In his cries to God, Job begs only to be in communion with God once again; Job does not beg for objects – God becomes his greatest desire.

What I have learned through all of my trials is that I don't need all the "toys" to have joy. They are nice to have, but they don't bring me real joy. My family and my health are what I really cherish, as Job did. Ultimately, the most important relationship in my life is the one I have with Jesus! I cannot live without Him, and I cannot have joy without Him. I need him more than anything in my life and God is enough!

Through it ALL, every single horrendous moment of his testing from Satan, Job remained blameless and did not sin against God. In the end, God blessed and prospered Job so much more than he could have ever imagined. Job lived in prosperity and a wonderful relationship with God for the remainder of his life. What a gift that would be!

Chapter 27

Visitor in the Night (June 2006, I.U. Medical Center)

The night before I was released to go home, I had a surprise visitor. It was about three in the morning, and I woke up with one of the Chinese residents on my surgical team staring into my face. He nearly scared me to death and he apologized for waking me, but said he just wanted to talk to me before I left the hospital the next day. He had tears in his eyes, and he held my hand. He said, "You taught me some things I never knew before." Then he just stood there holding my hand and staring at me.

I could tell he wanted to say more, but he was at a loss for words. I told him that he'd taught me something very special, too. "I was overwhelmed when you and the entire surgical team stood in my room with tear filled eyes because I would have to endure another surgery. It was then that I fully comprehended just how much each of you really care about ME! I was humbled to see the compassion and tenderness in the eyes, and on the faces of each of you. I am only here because of Jesus; He is the one true physician and healer. You have been blessed to be given all the tools and knowledge to do surgery, but the real healing comes from God." I was fighting to keep from crying, but now tears rolled down my cheeks.

He shook his head in agreement. We shared back and forth for a few moments longer, and then he left to finish his rounds. I thank God for His marvelous blessing that night.

"He makes the depths churn like a boiling caldron and stirs up the sea like a pot of ointment. Behind him he leaves a glistening wake; one would think the deep had white hair. Nothing on earth is his equal – a creature without fear. He looks down on all that are haughty; he is king over all that are proud" (Job 41:31-34).

Job truly understood the Mighty Power of God. God is the

Great I AM, and God alone deserves to be honored and glorified! Job feared and loved God. Job knew that God is just, and He alone can use all the insanity of Job's life for God's own glory. God alone would give Job the true joy he longed for.

God provided an excellent medical team for me, and He did His beautiful work through these surgeons. I know they'd been "picked out" for His perfect plan in my life to be carried out. How amazing is that? God used many different people to accomplish His plan, and my prayer is that persons associated with my medical situation who don't know Jesus Christ as their personal Lord and Savior will come to Him as a direct result of their seeing God's divine intervention in my life.

Chapter 28

Guilty as Charged (June 2006, I.U. Medical Center)

At times during my illness and recovery I was burdened with a tremendous amount of guilt. I felt guilty for not being a good mom. Both of my children were in college and struggling emotionally, and I desired more than anything to be available for them as I had in the past, but I simply was not. I didn't feel that I was a good wife to Larry. He never complained, and he was a pillar of strength for me; still, I felt I should have been more of a help and encouragement for him. I hated that I was responsible for causing our family to plunge into staggering financial debt. While it was nothing I could control, I knew I was the reason for the debt. Try as I might, I found myself lacking in my faith at times. I never blamed God for my situation or cursed Him. I wasn't bitter or angry at God, but I did question my situation and wondered if somehow I had disappointed God to the point that I deserved such punishment. Finally, I had tremendous guilt about not being a good support to my family, Larry's family, and his mother as she lay dying in the hospital. I felt somehow I should have done something, anything, to be more of a support. Much of the guilt was completely unwarranted, but I knew I fell prey to Satan's wicked attempts to keep me off-kilter and frustrated.

I expected that Job, a man found blameless and upright, should have many faithful friends – especially friends who would stand beside him and encourage him in a time of deepest need. I also expected that Job would not succumb to the pressures of guilt when he knew his heart was pure.

Job's friends, the very men he worshiped with, turned out to be his biggest adversaries, as they refused to show Job mercy. Who were these men who believed they were privy to such wisdom? Why did their prayers continue to accuse Job and cause him so much guilt and pain? Had these men used this opportunity to displace their own guilt onto Job? Job questioned himself and his motives all the time, and he felt condemned without sufficient warrant. He must have felt a tremendous amount of guilt as he could not convince his friends that his heart was pure, and that he honestly did not know why these horrific attacks were hurled against him.

I have felt similar condemnation and guilt when well-meaning Christians voice their judgment of me. They accused me of lacking in my faith, of having unconfessed sin in my life; once I was even questioned regarding the certainty of my salvation. How sad that Job was judged so harshly by his friends, and how cruel that any of us should be judged by anyone but God! Can these accusers read our minds or see inside the deeper caverns of our hearts? Only God knows man's thoughts and conscience. How, then, is it that we should be judged by man?

"Listen carefully to my words; let your ears take in what I say. Now that I have prepared my case, I know I will be vindicated. Can anyone bring charges against me? If so, I will be silent and die" (Job 13:17-19).

Although Job remained faithful to God and did not sin in what he said, it was very difficult for him to disregard his friends' flurry of accusations. Guilt and bitterness plagued him. He treasured God's Word – the living Bread of God. Because he treasured God's Word, Job knew he had to keep his focus on God if he wanted to find any kind of peace.

Much of my guilt concerning my family was self-inflicted and, with God's help, I was able to work through most of that fairly quickly. I wanted so badly to be able to care for my family as I had before. Satan worked overtime to try to destroy my faith and love for God. I kept trying to refocus. I needed to keep my mind on God, and I needed His staid peace in my heart!

"How much more, Lord, must I endure? I didn't even get the opportunity to see my mother-in-law before she died, and I couldn't attend her funeral." It was several months since I'd last seen Lois, and I missed her so. "God, I don't understand!" I received no answers except a mighty dose of comfort. I sensed God himself wrapped me in His strong, yet loving, arms and I never wanted to leave His embrace. How gracious and mighty is our God even when we don't understand His ways! How could I not praise Him?

How could Job not praise God even while mourning the loss of his family? As I said, I did not expect to experience accusations from fellow Christians. We are human and sometimes blurt out words we should never say. I should not have allowed those comments to affect me, but the truth is I did, and it hurt. I mean really hurt! We all lack in our faith at some point, and we all have sin. That's a given. Once more, I had to refocus, and I needed to keep my eyes on Christ. He would lead me in the right direction.

As did Job, I knew that I was doing my best to be faithful, and I trusted more in Christ than I ever had. Yes, I had sin, but if there was unconfessed sin causing me to be so ill, I was not aware of specifics. I had to be sure that I had not offended God without confession. I didn't want sin to separate me from my Jesus.

The most troubling comment was the remark that I was not saved. I knew then and know now, without a doubt, that I belong to God! He holds me in the palm of His hand, and NO ONE can pluck me from His hand. End of story! I was challenged to remember Jesus' immeasurable sacrifice on the cross and to move past the guilt of my accusers, including myself, to trust completely that God is in control, and He has covered my sin once and for all.

God showed me that each time I questioned His forgiveness, I crucified Jesus. Learning to let go of the guilt and clinging to the promises of God provide liberty, which is the epitome of freedom from guilt. I praise God for His endless mercy and grace! As I contemplate the events concerning my surgeries, the death of my mother-in-law and my other bouts of guilt, I can see now what I couldn't see then. God has extended His mercy and grace, He has forgiven me of my sins, and He shields me as I lie distraught and wounded. He has restored my soul and has breathed in me a new hope and desire to go on. He has made me new, refreshed me, made me wiser, and more dedicated to His work. I am more thankful than ever for every difficult, but good, situation that comes my way. Thank You, Lord.

Chapter 29

Guilt Multiplied (June 2006, I.U. Medical Center)

It was time to fill out the dreaded FAFSA forms for Sam and Meg and their universities. We didn't qualify for any financial aid, and it seemed ridiculous to go through this every year. It just made me so perturbed knowing we would have to take out more loans. I didn't know how we were going to pay them back with my not working, and I was even more worried that the loan administrators might not let us have any more loans because I wasn't working.

Family and friends reading this book might be shocked to know how badly my children struggled in college. They put on such a face of strength that not many people realized the absolute torment and frustration they lived in during a great part of their college years. I will never forget the long and deep conversations we had when Sam and Megan came home. We talked into the wee hours of the morning. They had so many questions, so many dilemmas, and they were hurting physically and emotionally. At times I was so exhausted that I could barely hold my head up, but I needed to be there for my children. I was so thankful, so VERY THANKFUL, for those precious times that our children let me into their private world and confided in me about how badly they hurt. We shared lots of tears, but most of the time we ended up with a moment of laughter, and we always prayed before our conversation was over. Even now, they revert to their forced smiles and pretend the struggle was all a bad dream. Both children had full-time credit hours, they worked all summer, and they worked during the school year. Work-study was not an unfamiliar term to them!

Megan studied Pre-Med, and she worked twenty hours a week as a personal assistant to one of the professors. She also babysat or worked as a nanny twenty to thirty hours a week for several of the doctors in Indianapolis. Sam studied to be a Physical Education teacher. During school he worked forty hours a week in sales for a fitness facility. He also had mandatory hours he had to spend observing in the classroom at the local elementary and high schools. Sam and Meg were completely stretched to their limits, were constantly exhausted, and too often sick! They never had time to rest, let alone study.

Megan contracted mononucleosis in her senior year of college, and it was only by the grace of God that she made it through that year. The doctors she worked with were a blessing we never expected. They watched out for her, encouraged her, and took her under their care. Megan also had wonderful friends and roommates who supported her. When I prayed for Megan, I never forgot to pray for those doctors and friends who were so good to her. I am still amazed that she managed to keep a 3.75 to 3.9 grade point average all through school.

While we were incredibly proud of our children for working so hard, Larry and I felt overwhelmed with guilt, and we wished we had the money to help them, so they would not have had to work so many hours. They missed so many wonderful experiences on campus and special events because they worked, slept, or caught up on homework.

Sam managed to keep decent grades, but they would have been so much better if he had not been working so many hours. If he sat down for any length of time, he'd fall asleep in his chair. When he did manage to come home, he'd fall asleep at the dinner table! Still, God was with them through it all and protected them. Both children are saved and this, of course, is a huge comfort to us. No one could have dreamed that at this time in their lives, when they were supposed to be embracing the golden opportunity of education in their desired profession, focusing on their studies, making lots of friends, having fun, and becoming mature and independent adults, it would be so traumatic. It wasn't fair, and they certainly did not deserve it. We didn't either, but praise God, He pulled us through.

As if their work schedules and classes were not enough stress, Megan and Sam were both very burdened with constant worry about me. I tried to shelter them from as much as I could, but at the bottom line, they were slammed with one tragedy after another. We hated it. Many nights Larry and I would be in tears as we prayed for our children, and we asked God to prevent all the unspeakable adversities they endured from permanently damaging them physically and emotionally. There was nothing more we could do, yet it was devastating to watch our children struggle. I called them frequently, but I wasn't sure if the calls made the situation better or worse. I needed to hear their voices to make sure they were all right. Megan was a freshman in 2006 and Sam was in his junior year of college. Both young adults, yes, but I still regarded them as my "babies," and I'll always be their mother.

In spite of all their difficulties, they did have lots of laughter and amusement thanks to their friends and family. It was so refreshing and comforting to hear stories of enjoyable times they spent hanging out with their friends. Although the merriment wasn't as often as they or I would have liked, it kept them level-headed and lightened the heavy burdens they bore. I loved to see the pictures on their cell phones or in Meg's scrapbooks as they laughed with their friends and entertained themselves. They needed pleasurable distraction in the worst way.

Even when they were just growing up, I never really allowed Sam and Meg to have much of a pity party. I wasn't going to tolerate their carrying on unless it involved a serious matter. Yes, they did their share of whining, but I really did try to cut it off as soon as I could. I always told them, "You'll be fine. Just shake it off and let's go." The longer they felt sorry for themselves, the more the chance they would have serious problems. I encouraged them to "slap on a smile" and keep going, even if they had to pretend.

My personal experience of happy pretense made good practice for actual happiness. Somewhere between the pretense and the actuality of being happy, I began to lose interest in the way I felt when I was angry. I didn't get the kind of attention I wanted when I whined, and crying over spilled milk certainly didn't make me happy either. I seemed to reach the "happy" point much quicker if I just yanked myself up and stopped thinking about the troublesome circumstances that just happened. I didn't have to pretend very long, because that encouragement of focusing on the positive caused me to be honestly happy. I think my children learned early on how that simple exercise allowed them to find peace even when they faced difficult times. It also kept others from knowing just how discontented they really felt. I didn't realize until I was an adult and came to know Jesus as my Savior that what I did is biblical.

Finally, brothers, whatever is true, whatever is noble, whatever is right, whatever is pure, whatever is lovely, whatever is admirable – if anything is excellent or praiseworthy – think about such things (Philippians 4:8-9).

Choosing to be happy allows us to move past the negativity and achieve the peace and "good stuff" much quicker. If I had my way, I'd omit the negative part completely, every single time, but I am human. I'm hard-headed at times, and I don't always follow my own advice. However, when I am having a difficult time, I do try to focus on that which is "true" and "noble" as we are directed in Philippians. After a few moments of reflecting on the good God has done in my life, I begin to feel more at peace with my situation. It doesn't mean it's all over or the situation is immediately remedied. It simply means I am able to be more at peace, and I can let go of the negative feelings that might otherwise engulf me. I wonder if Job ever used this simple exercise. He may not have even known he was practicing being positive, but I'm sure he did. Yes, he experienced all the normal emotions and feelings of anger or angst about his situation and the lack of his friends' compassion. Fortunately, Job reflected on a time when friends were comforted by his own words of kindness and a warm smile as he counseled them.

"After I had spoken, they spoke no more; my words fell gently on their ears. They waited for me as for showers and drank in my words as the spring rain. When I smiled at them, they scarcely believed it; the light of my face was precious to them. I chose the way for them and sat as their chief; I dwelt as a king among his troops; I was like one who comforts mourners" (Job 29:22-25).

"Even now my witness is in heaven; my advocate is on high.

My intercessor is my friend as my eyes pour out tears to God; on behalf of a man he pleads with God as a man pleads for his friend" (Job 16:19-21).

In his bitterness; having the hideous sores and his body clothed with scabs and worms, Job reflects on what he knows is good and just. He finds solace knowing that God is his friend and judge. Job fondly remembers how his old friends felt about him, and how he defended them, just as he knew God would defend him now. Job befriended men who needed and longed for words of encouragement as they sat in his counsel. The men remained speechless because Job understood the healing power of a warm smile as he showed so much compassion towards them. Job expected that same kind of compassion from his friends who were with him now. He asked these friends to plead to God on his behalf, but they refused. He received no words of comfort for his wearied soul from these earthly men. Job found that those he thought were friends fell short. Fortunately, God always comes to set the record straight! This reflection on the matter provided Job sweet relief even as he agonized over his lot, and focusing on the hope of God allowed Job to experience a small window of comfort. For a brief moment he found peace.

We parents all have hopes and dreams for our children as they go away to college; however, basically the desires are similar. We pray they don't forget the values they've been taught, their Christian roots and, most importantly, their relationship with Jesus. We also pray they become confident, responsible, and independent adults. We pray the life lessons learned at college will be something which helps them achieve their dreams.

When children have a mostly positive experience at college it can be predicted that they will come away with a fairly good chance of being successful at their job and in life as a whole. But when young people constantly face challenging problems or adversities throughout most of their college years, the outcome is a concern. The steady adversities that Megan and Sam faced could very easily have pushed them to turn away from God and exhibit a very bitter personality. Anger and frustration could have hardened their hearts against God, as well as against Larry and me. They could have turned to alcohol or drugs as a means to escape their mountain of troubles, and they could very easily have just dropped out of school. I believe a lot of young people would have.

Sam and Meg are not the only students who have endured repeated tribulations while attending college. It could have been much worse and we know that, but at the time our children were undeniably distressed. They had no idea how they would be able to deal with their ordeals, but God gave them the strength and courage to keep going. He never left their side, just as He never left my side.

It made me physically sick to think about the mounting debt hanging over our heads from the college loans. Larry and I began to talk about ways to cut back even more. We reviewed our bills and considered every possible luxury we could eliminate. Out of all that we owed, it was tempting to quit tithing, but we came to know the wonderful blessing of giving. We also knew the pain of holding out on God, so we refused to withhold His money from Him. I am not bragging when I share that we continued to give our ten percent even when we did not have the money. Because God was so faithful in meeting all our needs, we didn't dare stop now. We paid our tithes first, and what was left was used to pay bills until the money ran out. We trusted God that He would continue to supply our needs, and He did not disappoint us. When we "let go and let God," He replaced our fear and worry with joy and peace!

Chapter 30

Bowel Rest (July 2006, Home)

The bowel rest was extremely hard! No, not having anything to eat or drink for seventy-five days was more than hard, it was brutal. Every time I saw a food commercial or smelled food my mouth drooled, and I had to get away from the temptation. I know there are millions of children and adults going without food on a daily basis, and they have no promise of a meal. When they do eat, it's not a hot or nutritional meal as I would have, and they don't have clean water to drink. For the first time, I really understood what starvation felt like.

The junior and senior high students at our church were participating in the annual "Thirty Hour Famine" event. As a junior high youth leader, I was really disappointed to miss this wonderful time with our youth. For several months leading up to the event, the young people raised over $3,500.00 to fight world hunger. They spent thirty hours at the church participating in various activities and service projects. The one surrender was food! The students were allowed to have juice and water, but nothing more, as they learned just how difficult it is to go without food. While this was only a voluntary fast, the students understood that for many people, the lack of food is forced due to famine. Additionally, to my surprise, the participants from the Thirty Hour Famine event came to my home for a visit. I saw this as a significant teaching opportunity, and it was good to share with the youth just how difficult it is to go without food or drink for an extended time. God opened another door to allow me to share my adversities, my blessings, and how God sustained me through it all.

God refreshed my soul daily – not with food and drink, but with His living water that truly quenches the spirit. I was ecstatic to see how God used my weakened physical condition to strengthen my Christian resolve.

As I said, it was seventy-five days before I was allowed to have liquids, and then another two full weeks before I could have solids. At my seventy-fifth day, I had a big chocolate shake! Yummy, it was scrumptious! When I could finally have solids, I headed straight to my favorite fast food establishment for a large sweet tea and a Big Mac! That was not a good choice, but it was all I wanted; still, it made me really sick! I guess I just had to get it out of my system, and I certainly did, but not the way I intended. I can't even look at a Big Mac now without gagging.

"Does not man have hard service on earth? Are not his days like those of a hired man? Like a slave longing for the evening shadows, or a hired man waiting eagerly for his wages, so I have been allotted months of futility, and nights of misery have been assigned to me" (Job 7:1-3).

When we know there is an end in sight, we can endure; however, most of the time, we are not privy to knowing when the end will come or how long we must endure a hardship or problem. That's where faith steps in. We must believe, we must trust, and we must keep our eyes on the Lord. In the end, we will make our "Daddy God" very proud, and He loves it when we bring Him glory and honor. It's easy to be faithful when we know the outcome or can see enough to imagine the result, but what happens when we are totally unaware? Faith happens. We must step out in pure FAITH and let God do His work in us! The result is amazing!

I can do everything through him who gives me strength (Philippians 4:13).

The bowel rest was harder than I imagined, but God gave me the strength to make it through. When I was allowed to eat, the taste of food was exceptionally delicious. For Job, God sweetened the pot as well. When he passed the testing, God gave Job so much more than he ever expected. God is so good to us when we are faithful. Faith is rewarded!

Chapter 31

Is This a Test or What? (November 2007, Home)

At my follow-up appointment with Dr. Touloukian, he reminded me that my colostomy would be permanent. It wasn't what I originally wanted, but God changed my heart. I learned to appreciate the gift of my colostomy. After all, it is now a part of me, and it is keeping me alive. I depended on God to help me, and slowly but surely, I did adjust. It was not easy, and I have had some major challenges along the way because I have had more leaks than I care to discuss. On more than a dozen occasions, I have had a major blowout in public places.

One day my daughter Meg and I went to an expensive steak house for lunch. We were starved and really looking forward to a nice sit-down meal together. The restaurant's famous hot yeast rolls and sweet tea tasted so good, but I was really looking forward to my pecan encrusted chicken salad. I just finished my first glass of iced tea when the waitress came with our meals. As soon as she sat our meals on the table, I felt a super hot flash come over me. My stomach started cramping, and my colostomy bag completely filled in a matter of seconds!

The waitress could see something was wrong by the look on my face. I was relieved when she set the meals down and walked away. I didn't want to waste time explaining to her what was going on, because I just needed to get out of there as quickly as possible. I was in a panic! Meg really worried about what was about to take place. She was twenty-one years old, and thought she had all the answers. "Mom, just get up and walk slow...ly to the bathroom. You'll be fine if you just move really slow."

I love her, but she didn't have a clue! I didn't have time to argue with her, and I could tell I was going to embarrass her terribly, but I was in a lose – lose situation!

My colostomy bag was so full that I knew the slightest movement would break the seal and have me swimming in a horrible mess of "you know what!" I didn't know what to do. I just finished off a full glass of tea, so I knew I would have more liquid coming through very soon and there was nowhere for it to go. The additional pressure would blow the seal for sure. The bag was already so heavy that I knew the seal would blow if I moved even the slightest bit, and I would have no control over the mess that would follow. I had no options.

The worst case scenario played out, and I couldn't do a single thing to stop it. My next thought was how to make the quickest exit with the least amount of damage. We were seated in a booth about thirty feet from the front door. The bathroom was much farther away, and I would have to make several twists and turns around a full restaurant of people trying to enjoy their lunch. I opted for the front door.

I handed Meg my credit card and a twenty-dollar bill. "Meg, I am going to make a mad dash to the front door. I'll never make it to the bathroom. Don't argue with me, just please, listen! When I get out of here, call the waitress over and explain what happened. Give her this twenty-dollar tip, and tell her I am extremely sorry for the mess. Pay for the meals on my charge card and ask the waitress to put our food in "to go" boxes. Then meet me in the car just as soon as you can."

I didn't wait for a response from her. I just said a quick prayer and slid to the edge of the booth. The minute I stood up the flood gates opened up, and stool ran down my leg. I frantically tried to get to the front door, and as I was fleeing the restaurant, I left a trail of nasty stuff all over the nice tile floors all the way out the door! Talk about humiliating! Thank God, I didn't run into anyone coming into the restaurant as I escaped!

Meg was mortified and furious with the whole situation. I knew it would be a long, chilly ride home! I understood how she felt, but I just did not know what to do about it. All I could do was apologize, and that only seemed to make matters worse. I was in tears myself, and I was so angry that this happened and ruined our day out.

"Why, God? Why? Why does this always happen? Can't we just enjoy one solitary day out without any ordeals or tragedies?" I shouted my frustration to God as Meg sat silently in the front seat, refusing to look at me. Meg needed to vent, and I wanted to be really mad at her for not understanding, but I just couldn't. She tolerated far more than most twenty-one year olds ever would have, and I knew she loved me. I understood how she felt, and if the shoe were on the other foot, I'd feel the same way.

Megan started to cry. How was I going to console her, when I was literally up to my eyeballs in poop! I burst into tears, too. After a few moments, Meg turned around and started pulling supplies out of my bag to help me. She slung her arms all over the place, and her reddened face testified to her frustration.

All of a sudden, I burst out laughing and I could not stop! Here I was in the middle of a restaurant parking lot, stark naked in the back seat of Meg's car, covered in liquid stool, and I was laughing so hard I could barely breathe!

"Stop it. Don't you dare laugh! Mom, this is not funny! Do you hear me? This is not funny! You have no idea how embarrassing that was to tell the waitress, 'I'm sorry, my grown mother just had an accident and there is poop all over your nice, clean, expensive floors.' You should have seen her face!"

The problem was, I COULD imagine the look on the waitress' face and it made me laugh even more! I couldn't help myself and I just kept laughing. "Meg, think about it. You have to admit, this is funny! We might as well laugh instead of cry about this!" I just kept laughing and watching her face.

Slow...ly, I mean very slow...ly, there was a smile cracking her face. Then all at once she blurted out, "Okay, it is funny!" We laughed for several minutes before I could resume cleaning up the mess I was in. I thanked God over and over that I had my emergency bag in the car with a change of clothes and new colostomy supplies. We now worked together feverishly to get me cleaned up and changed and to make sure there was not a speck of anything on the seat of Meg's car. We were both absolutely exhausted from all the laughing, crying, and cleaning up the mess.

We were also starved. However, after cleaning up, neither

one of us could eat right then. We opened the "to go" boxes and found our salads wilted from the dressing. Meg took the boxes and dumped them in the trash just outside the restaurant doors. On the way home, we stopped at the drive-through of a fast-food place and got sandwiches to take home. What a day!

It took me a very long time, almost a year, to adjust to my colostomy, but I did eventually adjust. Today, when I have an accident, I am able to stay relatively calm. I can usually recover just fine without falling to pieces or sobbing like a baby. Most times I can even laugh about it.

As Le Barbier de Seville, IV said, "I quickly laugh at everything, for fear of having to cry."

"Does it please you to oppress me, to spurn the work of your hands, while you smile on the schemes of the wicked?" (Job 10:3).

Job could not imagine how God could be so angry with him. He began to believe that God was punishing him for some unknown or unconfessed sin, and Job felt he was toyed with. I felt that way on the day of my accident at the steakhouse. I hadn't been as embarrassed as I was that day in a very long time, and the circumstances were traumatic for both Megan and me.

When I look back, I am amazed at how quickly I recovered from the disaster. Within thirty minutes or so, the whole ordeal was over, I was completely cleaned up, and I was ready to go. The accident turned into a blessing, and I thanked God that we were able to come out of the "attitude" so easily and so quickly. I thanked God for Meg being there to help me, and I thanked God most of all for the gift of laughter!

Chapter 32

Oh, Happy Day (End of June 2006, I.U. Medical Center)

During my hospital stay to attempt a reversal of my colostomy, I had three different roommates. They were all very nice, but just as we would get to know each other and begin to connect, each would be released, and I'd get a new roommate. That was okay, because the last roommate was the best, and she was a lot of fun. She and I liked the same music, so I'd crank my CD player up and we'd listen to music all day long.

One of my friends, Joni, gave a CD to me a long time ago of Rod Stewart's music. It has "Moon River" and all of the "old classics" on it. When we weren't listening to praise and worship, my roommate would ask me to play the Rod Stewart CD.

The "Oldies but Goldies" made me think of my mom and dad: I especially missed my mom and her sympathetic demeanor. Mom and Dad have been gone for several years now, but I still envision them dancing around the floor to Nat King Cole's "Unforgettable." That was their favorite song. They loved to dance, and when we had family weddings, they always stole the show when they were on the dance floor.

Anyway, my roommate loved to tell jokes and act silly. We laughed and had so much fun just sharing stories. On one occasion the nurse lingered longer than usual after she took our vitals, and the nursing staff checked in on us more than usual. We could hear the doctors and nurses talking, like they were camped right outside our door.

When my roommate went for a walk, she said there were several doctors and nurses all hanging out around our door and cutting up. They were acting like they were dancing and talking about the jitterbug and the waltz.

We quizzed the nurses and asked them what they were doing out there.

Their response was, "Nothing, we just like hanging out with you young folk."

A little later one of the resident doctors came in to check me and said, "Hey, I here this is the happening place. Can you turn the music up a bit so we can hear it in the hall, if you don't mind?"

I looked at my roommate to make sure she was okay with it. She said, "Crank it up!"

So I did, and the doctor started dancing all around the room as if he had a partner. A nurse grabbed him, and they started dancing together. It was so odd, but cool!

That was the best therapy! It made our day, and it was enjoyable to see the nurses and doctors celebrate the moment as well. Such simple experiences as music and laughter can bring people together in ways never imagined, and it's an especially effective way to melt away stress. That was a wonderful day!

After Job suffered many atrocities, the Lord told Job that He was angry with his friends. They had not spoken of Him what was right, as Job had. Eliphaz would take his seven bulls and seven rams to God's servant, Job, and sacrifice a burnt offering for them. Job would pray for his friends, and God would accept Job's prayer and not deal harshly with his friends as they deserved. That's the mercy of God. The men did as God directed them, and the Lord accepted Job's prayer.

After Job prayed for his friends, the Lord prospered Job and gave him twice as much as he had before. All his brothers, sister, and everyone who had known him before came and ate with him in his house. They comforted Job over all that God brought him through. Each person gave Job a piece of silver and a gold ring.

In his later life, Job received even more of God's blessings. Job was particularly blessed with seven sons and three daughters, and his daughters were the most beautiful women in the land. Job gave all his sons and daughters an inheritance from his fourteen thousand sheep, six thousand camels, a thousand yoke of oxen, and a thousand donkeys. Job lived to be one hundred and forty years old, and he saw his children and their children to the fourth generation.

Because of his faithfulness and innocence, Job was found blameless despite Satan's testing. God blessed Job beyond all that he believed possible. It is difficult to imagine the celebration which took place in Job's home when he was finally vindicated! His friends were wrong, and God let them know it. I am sure Job was the happiest man in the world at that moment. No, he was not just happy – he had JOY – unspeakable JOY!

Chapter 33

Daily Struggles (2009 through 2010, Home)

I have been in and out of the hospital numerous times since my last surgery. I have suffered with all kinds of problems from heart issues, adhesions, bladder problems, migraines, blood clots, blood infection, dehydration, nose bleeds, insomnia, spondylosis, anxiety, and much more over the past six years. It seems to be a never-ending battle as I try to work my way back to health. I continue to pray for total healing, and I know God will honor my request, I just don't know when; all the while I see the dollar signs click, click, and click as the bills mount into the thousands. We pay as we can and continue to trust God will take care of us.

We had new neighbors move into our addition, and one day while Larry and I were out walking, our new neighbors asked us to come up onto their porch and visit. Gary, a part-time minister, and his wife, Kathy, were very nice to us. We stood there for a moment getting acquainted, and then the discussion took on a more serious tone.

I could feel the Spirit's presence, the Paraclete, the moment we stepped onto that porch. I am convinced that porch is a Holy place. As we talked, I learned of Gary's disability that caused him to lose the use of his legs. He is now confined to a wheelchair, and his condition, ALD, continues to worsen. He asked me all about my medical dilemmas, and we felt immediate connection – a bond that translated into praying for one another and a friendship that is very special.

He asked me, "What is the worst thing that you are afraid of in all of this?"

I thought for awhile and told him that I feared the humiliation and consequences of bankruptcy most. I didn't feel it was something God would want, and I was proud of the good credit rating we maintained. Just then, I realized that I had, and still have, a lot of pride.

In respect to finances, Gary said to me, "God will take you all the way down to your underwear if He has to. He wants your complete trust and humility." He was right! God still has a lot of work to do in me, and I am so thankful for friends like Gary and Kathy who were honest and loving in counseling with us.

Job was bold in his faith, but he was humble in spirit. Thomas Stearns Eliot said, "The only wisdom we can hope to acquire is the wisdom of humility; humility is endless." Job is wise in that he fears God, and his worship is that of praise and humility. I love God and I love to serve Him, but God wants more. He wants to strip away my ugly pride and expose a pure heart, humble before Him and man. To worship in true humility, as Job did, I must let go of my pride. God is preparing me for an eternity of worship where humility is endless, and my time here on earth is my "dress rehearsal."

I believe that in our most difficult times, God gives us refreshment. Refreshments are moments of revival, and can be unexpected blessings as well. I have probably missed out on the many surprises God planned for my refreshment, because my mind gets so focused on the mountain of adversities before me, that I literally miss the blessing right in front of my face! When I am in a situation that has me overwhelmed, that's when I need a touch from God most! He helps me to "regroup" and focus on Him.

I asked God to help me realize His gifts no matter how distracted I am. God answered my prayer. While the unexpected blessings often bring the most significant refreshment for me, God continues to remind me that I have constant blessings. I make a mental list of these. My family, shelter, food, friends and health insurance are just a few. These helps are not guaranteed, but they are, for the most part, constant! That's it – It is so ... SIMPLE! I decided to make small paper lists of my blessings that are "constants," and I carry a list in my purse, in my Bible, taped on my bathroom mirror, and stuck on my refrigerator. These are all "places" I visit quite often.

These constants become the refreshment I long for. I realize I am never, ever without a blessing, and God provides a means for me to be revived and to refocus in a matter of seconds. Of course, I still appreciate the unexpected blessings sprinkled throughout my life, because they are new and different, but I already have the consistent blessings in my life, and I have learned the value of those simple, reliable helps!

I remember a very difficult day when my colostomy constantly leaked. I had already changed my appliances twice that day, my skin was getting irritated, and I was pushed to the point of tears. When the seal broke for a third time, I was so upset that I asked God to please help me refocus, because I knew a negative attitude would get me nowhere.

I started thinking about one of the constants in my life, Larry, and how much he truly loves me. I remembered how compassionate he is, and how he can always make me laugh. I felt the frustration slowly fade, and I even let a smile come over my face. Without even realizing it, I was immediately refreshed by an unexpected blessing.

On the way to the bathroom to change my colostomy appliances again, I saw my mail on the table that I hadn't opened yet. I came across an envelope from a hospital in Columbus, Indiana. When I opened it I found it was a letter from a colostomy support group at the hospital. I didn't even know there were support groups for colostomy patients! That was no coincidence! Inside the envelope was a newsletter, and I found an article about a new colostomy appliance which would be very effective in reducing, and perhaps even eliminating, leaks! The appliance is called "Barrier Ring," and my colostomy supplier carried it! Suddenly, I realized the unexpected blessing! God supplied instant refreshment for me, but God didn't stop there. He is so good!

Also inside the envelope was a sample "Barrier Ring." I took the ring, the instructions, and I went to work. In a matter of minutes I had the new appliance in place! For the very first time in a long while, I was able to get a very good seal with the appliance. I wondered how long the seal would last since it seemed to be so secure. If this worked as well as the article claimed it would, it could save both money and aggravation. I called my supplier right away and ordered several more Barrier Rings.

The seal held so well that I did not have to change my colostomy appliances for another four days! That was a miracle, since I had been changing my appliance almost everyday, and sometimes more than once a day. I thanked God for His wonderful refreshment that day!

Chapter 34

A Very Special Blessing (May 2010, Home)

One Sunday afternoon I was sick in bed, when Larry came and told me that nearly one hundred church members, family, and friends were gathered outside our home. I asked him what was going on and why they were there. He said people from our church, First Baptist, and others who wanted to come and pray for us were making the visit. Instantly, I was upset. "You know I don't feel good. Are all those people coming in the house? I look terrible! Why didn't you ask me first?" I couldn't believe that Larry had invited all those people when I was sick! I felt really awful for complaining that way, but I just was not up to entertaining anyone!

Larry fell silent, and the most pitiful look came over his face. Before he could answer, the door bell rang and my brother Jim and his wife, Gloria, came in. They were so excited to see the big turn out. Gloria knew I was sick, but she was surprised to know that I had a 102 degree temperature. She explained a little more about what was going on outside, and she assured me that no one would come in. Thankfully, I didn't need to worry about entertaining anyone. All of the visitors in my front yard were there simply to pray for me and my family. They surrounded our home and covered every inch of our property with love and prayers. They took us to the very throne of God!

What a wonderful surprise! I wished I felt better so I could go out and thank them and be a part of the prayer circle. Gloria told me to stay in bed, however, and I wouldn't even be bothered. Honestly, I didn't have the energy to get out of bed even if I wanted to.

After our friends spent over forty-five minutes praying for us, they came to my bedroom window, and Larry returned to our bedroom and told me our visitors would like to sing. Larry wanted to know if he could open the bedroom window so I could hear them.

Larry opened the window and fresh summer air filled the room. It felt so good, and a huge choir began to sing the most beautiful songs. Larry sat beside me on the bed as we listened. I love music because it touches the very heart of me and is so soothing. I remember them singing "Trading My Sorrows," "How Great is Our God," and several other worship songs. I honestly felt I was in heaven listening to the angels sing. I closed my eyes, and I could see Jesus smiling at me with angels all around Him.

Don't stop! They finished singing and whispered good-byes as they walked away. It was the most beautiful experience I'd had in a very long time, and I didn't want them to leave! They gave me the most incredible gift of love, and I will never forget that day! Larry and I had tears rolling down our cheeks.

We asked each other, "What did we ever do to deserve this magnificent blessing?"

We couldn't speak. The emotion overtook us ... and we just held each other and sobbed with immense gratitude. God loves us so much. He gives us mercy and grace instead of what we really deserve, and He fills our hearts with so much peace and joy. There are no words to thank Him for all He continues to do in our lives.

As a result of God's gift of love, I have a new passion for those in need of prayer. Through His guidance, God helps me with a ministry I call the Prayer Gathering, for lack of a better name right now. We are "praying forward" the intense necessity of intercessory prayer. While it's still a fairly new ministry, many blessings have come for both the prayer warrior and the recipient. As it is with all adversities in life, God makes something good of what seems so negative. He is faithful and just, and He delivers! My recovery was difficult, but not impossible. I cling to my faith, and my relationship with Jesus grows stronger and more precious to me day by day.

After all Job endured, he passed Satan's test. Job was found blameless and faithful.

The Lord Himself said this to Eliphaz the Temanite, *"... My servant Job will pray for you, and I will accept his prayer and not deal with you according to your folly. You have not spoken of me what is right, as my servant Job has" (Job 42:8).* After Job prayed for his friends, God prospered Job.

I find it ironic that Job became the mediator for his friends – the very friends who accused and tormented him by insisting Job had unconfessed sin. He suffered immeasurable torture and losses, and he questioned why God allowed such torture; but he never cursed God or sinned against Him. After all of Job's trials, he was found blameless. Job's prayer for his friends and their sacrifice were the means of forgiveness for them.

Jesus is the mediator between us and God. Jesus is our Redeemer and Friend, and yet we accuse Him, mock Him, and crucify Him. Jesus, even in His human form and tortured as He was, did not sin. Jesus was completely blameless and sinless.

I'm not implying that Job is on the same level with Jesus, but he did pass a remarkable test – one that even the most seasoned Christians would fail. He did become the mediator between his friends and God. In all of the horrible testing, Job remained blameless and sinless. Honoring God is the essential value of such a testing. Job evidenced an amazing faith and love for God.

Chapter 35

The Great Invention (July 2008, Home)

In the later months of 2008, I was home recovering and doing fairly well, but I began experiencing increased bouts of dehydration and malnutrition. I routinely emptied my colostomy bag ten to fifteen times a day. I became weaker and experienced more physical problems. My hair and skin dried, and I began having daily nosebleeds. I was extremely tired and suffered daily headaches, and at least once or twice a week I had a migraine headache.

My colostomy worked overtime, and I often had episodes of "dumping syndrome." Everything I ate or drank immediately emptied into my colostomy bag. Food didn't have time to digest, and I could not absorb the nutrients I needed. I avoided restaurants like the plague, because I never had enough time to make it home after I ate without having to stop along the way to empty my bag. The home health nurses started coming again, and I infused 1000 cc's of IV fluids a day to compensate for my constant dehydration. Eventually, the fluids were decreased to every other day.

Besides being completely drained and exhausted from the dehydration, I was not getting adequate sleep. Since my surgery in January of 2006, there was not a single night without my having to get up to the bathroom at least seven or eight times to empty my colostomy bag!

My brother Dan is both intelligent and inventive. I knew if anyone could help me, he could. I asked Dan to create a system that would be compatible with my colostomy appliance and would act as a collection station for my massive amount of output. I desperately wanted to be able to sleep through the night! I also needed a system that I could easily maneuver, along with my IV pole, in case I needed to go to the bathroom during the night. To complicate matters, I had a five-pound limit on what I could lift.

Dan asked me questions as to how my colostomy is attached, how it empties, and how I manage to sleep even though I continually empty the small bag. He took samples of all my supplies home and went to work developing a system that would allow me the sleep I needed.

In a matter of days, Dan designed a thin, wide, long, plastic tubing that flared into a very large pouch which could hold almost a gallon of fluid. It's a one-piece system and weighs less than eight ounces. At the end of the pouch, the large opening folds down and is secured by a tight clip.

The apparatus attaches to the flange on my abdomen and the large pouch rests in a five gallon bucket in case any part of the pouch springs a leak. The five gallon bucket rests on a wooden platform at the base of the IV pole, making it all one system. Since the IV pole has wheels, it is possible to maneuver the IV fluids, tubing, and the colostomy system with ease and avoid any dangerous lifting issues.

I have no idea how Dan came up with a solution so quickly. I just know that God not only blessed me with a wonderful brother, He gave me the added bonus of a brother who is very gifted. God has used Dan to help me in so many ways, and I have been, and continue to be, forever blessed because of him.

Dan's wife, Deanna, made a removable cloth cover for the colostomy system and a separate cover that fits snugly over the top of the five gallon bucket the system rests in. All of the apparatus is completely concealed and odorless. Incredible! I still use Dan's invention today when I encounter flare-ups with diarrhea or dumping syndrome. Dan and Deanna will never know the full impact of their blessing for me.

I asked God to help me with all my health struggles and God gave me the help I needed to get through. He was with me in the trenches and He's never left me! He made it so I could focus on Him and not the pain or myself – that doesn't mean it was "pretty," but I did make it through with His help and His abundant mercy.

All along God provided me with hope. I really have no excuse for my questioning and occasional doubts. Perhaps it should have been much easier for me to be faithful with all the glimpses of hope I have been privy to, but I wondered – did God know I might fail without those glimmers of hope? I pray not. It is my honest desire to be faithful in all situations, good or bad.

Job was not so fortunate to be privy to such evidence of hope. He did not have the luxury of knowing how God would send Jesus to become human, suffer defeat temporarily on the cross, and then prove victory forever at the cross! For Job, hope seemed farther away as his plight continued, and he had no idea when his suffering would end. He truly walked through the entire ordeal with pure faith, and he leaned heavily on God to keep him sane. Even as he questioned God, Job did not sin against God, nor did he charge God. Job remained faithful in light of no signs of relief. Faith is belief in something without seeing it, and Job is an example of the best in human nature.

Chapter 36

Dire Straits (May 2009 to March 2010, Home)

Larry and I found ourselves in dire straits and we needed to sell our home so we could get out from under the large house payments. We knew we were only a payment away from foreclosure, but there was nothing more to sell, no other services we could drop, and no one to loan us any more money. The real estate market bottomed out, and we found ourselves facing a loss as we priced our home to sell. We owed far more than our home was worth, and for three years we prayed for a buyer, but none came, and I could not understand why our home didn't sell.

Then one day my whole world came crashing down. We realized that it was time for us to get help and see what legal options we might have regarding our finances. Larry was not able to go with me to talk to the attorney, so I went by myself. Although I refused bankruptcy, I knew that was the option the attorney would most likely suggest, and I was right. I was so rattled I could barely focus on what the attorney told me. As the attorney talked I looked straight at him, but I did not comprehend a single word he said. I was never as uncomfortable in my life as I was sitting in that office; I felt I was being swallowed up, and I could barely breathe. I never wanted to file bankruptcy. I still had fight in me and trusted God to be in control. I just wanted to get home and crawl in a hole so no one could see or speak to me. I was ashamed and feared I had betrayed my trust in God somehow in talking with the attorney. As I poured my heart out to God, I begged for His intervention in our finances.

I wasn't home very long, maybe twenty minutes, before God invoked a miracle. He provided both our rescue and the individuals to make it happen. I was shocked and could not believe what God did. Humbled and unworthy of this very generous gift of help … I could only thank God for His unbelievable mercy.

The servants God used to bless us truly love God, and that is why it is so important that they remain anonymous, so God alone is glorified. Their church took us on as one of their missions. Aware of our deep dependence and devotion to God, they only required that we continue to serve Him and be witnesses in the community – missionaries in our locality. I'd been sending "updates" to hundreds of people about my illness, my journey with God, and His working in our lives, and the anonymous benefactors suggested these updates could be an effective mission. The short messages might be a way to encourage others and to glorify God in all that we were experiencing.

I had never thought about God using me as a missionary, and as a result, I was humbled and overwhelmed. In Matthew 28, Christians are commissioned to go into all the world and preach the gospel to all nations. That's what missionaries do. They give up everything to GO where God sends them to share the gospel of Jesus Christ with those who don't know Him.

I prayed about what being a missionary would really mean in my life, and God showed me that He needed me, right here in Greensburg, Indiana. Being a missionary simply means being willing to GO and share the gospel. God might take us overseas, but usually that's not the case. God calls the majority of us to be missionaries in our own backyards, and there are plenty of opportunities!

God has performed so many miracles in my life, and I cannot keep silent regarding all He has done in me. He continually blesses me and my family, He gives me real JOY in the midst of much turmoil, and He has CHANGED MY LIFE COMPLETELY! I am passionate about sharing my story of God's grace and mercy. Sometimes I feel so unworthy of the blessings Larry and I enjoy; there are times, I think I am not very encouraging, and I question my adequacy to be His missionary. All I can do is trust God to continually work in Larry and me, and let others see Him in us. We pray that the simple seeds of faith we plant through our testimonies help change lives for Him. We are so blessed and thankful for all that God has done for us. We still marvel at God's orchestration.

Larry and I hoped we could sell our home and make a small profit so we could pay off some of our debt. That was not God's plan. I still had too much pride, and God taught me complete humility. While we needed to sell the home to eliminate the big payments, the goal was not to make a profit off the backs of another family looking for an affordable home. The goal was to get the relief we needed and pass the blessing on to the next person.

Our realtor, Andrea, is a Christian, and she was a significant part of God's plan in the selling of our home. We are thankful for what she accomplished, and how well she worked with the other realtor to sell our home during the housing crisis. The sale of homes was in gridlock, and that was further confirmation that God was totally in control of the sale of our home. When we finally sold our home, we walked away from the closing with a profit of 500 dollars! God is so good!

We never divulged the sources of our help, as they have requested, but we have repeatedly shared the story of how God made a way for us to keep our home until it sold. It all happened in His perfect timing, not ours! God's glory was evident in the entire process, and I know the ones who helped us were blessed as well.

The young couple who bought our home has a baby, and they love their new home. They have already made some wonderful changes, which have improved the value of the home, and I am so glad they are taking such good care of it. The day we closed, I stopped by their home to show them where the key could be found to the shut off valve on the gas fireplace. Before I left, the couple allowed me the honor of praying with them. I asked for God's blessing on their new home and for God to bless their family.

When Job prayed for his friends to receive mercy instead of getting what they deserved, it reminded me of how special it feels to pray for others. None of us deserve the grace and mercy we receive, because we all have sin and disappoint God every day. I wanted this new family to know God's blessings, and I also wanted them to know God's unlimited bounty. Truly, I want everyone to know God's grace and mercy. It's an honor and blessing to pray for our family, friends, and for those God puts in our paths.

Chapter 37

Bowel Transplant
(July 2009, I.U. Medical Center, Out Patient)

In the midst of all our financial trouble, I was considered for a bowel transplant; I was both excited and scared to death! A successful transplant would certainly improve my life and, although I had no idea how we'd pay for it, I would follow God's leading and trust Him to take care of the details.

Years earlier, multiple organ transplants were required for the procedure, but now there was new technology that made it possible for surgeons to do the bowel transplant by itself. The transplant was still extremely dangerous, and the possible complications were frightening. I had "casually" asked my surgeon about a transplant a couple of years earlier, but he said I was not a candidate unless it became a matter of life and death. Now, there was renewed hope, and the bowel transplant seemed a real possibility.

I knew the expense could be in the millions of dollars, but to my surprise, my insurance paid 100% of all the transplant pre-testing! I had a very thorough work up and exam, and I mean thorough!

Doors opened, and we began trusting these opportunities as the "go ahead" from God. We completely trusted that God was in control.

Following the testing, I met with one of the transplant surgeons. There were many concerns and questions whirling through my mind, and the surgeon spent over an hour answering all of my questions. He also discussed many concerns I hadn't thought about. The surgeon shared that in 2005 the transplant team at I.U. Medical Center was awarded the Center of Excellence Award, and the survival rate for intestinal transplant patients at year three was eighty-nine percent.

The transplant surgeon and I talked about the cost, issues with insurance, timing, concerns with my current health status, required labs, follow-up visits, anti-rejection drugs, a four to five months follow-up surgery and, most importantly, the risks. The surgeon has many transplant patients who are now leading perfectly normal lives, yet, this would not be something to go into lightly, and there would be no guarantees.

Wow! This was a lot to consider! A transplant is a very delicate surgery and one that needs to be considered with much prayer. I was excited at the thought of being well again, but the risk of something going wrong was frightening! On one hand, I feared moving ahead, and on the other hand, I knew God would stop this process immediately if it was not to be. I definitely needed lots of prayer, as did every surgeon on the transplant team.

The next step involved a review of all test results, getting findings of all my exams, and then making a final decision whether or not to do the transplant. The final decision to do the very complicated and dangerous transplant would be made after a team of surgeons and other doctors presented all their findings. The surgeon said it could be weeks before he would get all of the team back together for their feedback.

He was right. For several weeks I prayed and wondered what the decision might be. My life was on hold, and then out of the blue, I got the call. The decision was made, and the surgeons all agreed that I was NOT to have the transplant! I tortured myself with worry over the decision, believing it was mine to make. But fortunately, our infinite God of mercy took care of that for me. It was His decision to make, and He made that quite evident as He worked in and through those surgeons reviewing my case.

"Praise the Lord!" I almost shouted it out loud! I was so relieved! At least I knew now that I was not to have the transplant and I could move on with my life.

The transplant team's decision was based on the fact that I was still fairly young and doing very well, considering all I had been through. The complications from a transplant might severely compromise what little "good" health I was experiencing. I was able to spend time with family and get out to do light shopping and other errands. Given all my current medical conditions, a transplant raised a critical concern that I might end up spending the rest of my life in a long-term care facility. There were too many variables to take such a risk at this time.

Thank You, Jesus, for watching over me!

Chapter 38

One More Surgery (January 2010, I.U. Medical Center)

In January of 2010, I went to my local emergency room because of severe low abdominal pain. This was my third trip to the ER in five weeks, and I worried the ER doctors would think I was making up the pain and symptoms, because they were unable to find the source of my pain, or the reason I was having little to no output from my colostomy. Believe me, I was feeling much more frustrated than the doctors! The ER doctor asked all sorts of questions and promised he'd get to the bottom of it. He ordered a CAT scan, did some labs, and he came back an hour or so later with some news.

"We have the CAT scan report, but it does not show anything to really help us. I just have this feeling we may find something if we run a second CAT scan with contrast. Your insurance might not pay for it, but I really feel we might get a better idea of what's going on. Are you willing?"

We did not have the money to pay for another scan, but I needed help and I really did trust this doctor. It was evident to me that he did care and he might find the answers we needed. I agreed and was wheeled back to the X-ray department for another scan.

Praise the Lord! The second CAT scan paid off. The doctor came back with the results.

"Well, we have our answer. It might not be what you want to hear, but we know what's going on now. You have a softball size hernia pushing against the bowel and blocking stool from getting to the colostomy. What's the name of your surgeon? I am going to give him a call and make arrangements for you to be transferred to I.U. Medical Center so he can follow-up with you there."

Wow, this certainly was not what I expected. I was shocked! Dr. Touloukian had already told me that he could not do any more surgeries. The adhesions were excessive, and there was a very high risk of organ damage or even death. How would he get to the hernia without doing some major damage to other organs and the small amount of bowel I had left?

If Dr. Touloukian couldn't operate, what would happen to me? Will the surgeon just let me lie there until the bowel ruptures and I die? Is surgery imminent and will I die in the process anyway? Larry was scared. He followed the ambulance to Indianapolis amid a looming sense of urgency, yet no one, not even the ambulance crew, seemed to be in a hurry. I was admitted right away and, to my surprise, taken directly to my room. I didn't see my surgeon until the next day.

Larry wanted answers, so he came to the hospital very early the following morning, but it was almost 9:00 a.m. before Dr. Touloukian came in. He was visibly upset with the news, and he did not want to do surgery. He reminded us how risky surgery would be due to my many adhesions and the condition of my intestines. He said he was going to consult with his surgical team to see if they could brainstorm a way to help me. In the meanwhile, I could not leave the hospital. Dr. Touloukian said he'd get back with us, but it would take some time for him to get all of his team together, and we needed to be patient. So, we waited.

It's never good to see a surgeon struggle with the decision to operate, but this time it really did unnerve me. I didn't know if I even had that option. If I did, would I survive it? I didn't know if I had it in me to go through this again. I was so tired, and I hated that Larry, Megan, and Sam would have to deal with this again, too. All I knew to do was pray.

Finally, the verdict was in – Dr. Touloukian and his team made the decision to operate. Without the surgery I would die, and with the surgery I had a shaky 50/50 chance of survival. "Without surgery I would die?" I was shocked!

Dr. Touloukian said he planned to "take down" my colostomy and remove the hernia through the old colostomy site to avoid getting into as much of the adhesion network as he could. Then he would relocate the colostomy just under my left rib cage. This was an area that had not previously been involved with any tissue or organ manipulation, so it was relatively free of adhesions. The process was very risky, but was my only hope for survival.

I still had so many unanswered questions, and later that day Larry said the surgeon called him and wanted to set up a meeting with the family to discuss the surgery. Maybe this would help me to be more comfortable with the whole situation. I knew in my heart I was not going to die, but I was really concerned about the results of the surgery and what my quality of life might be.

Two days later, Dr. Touloukian met with my family in my hospital room. The surgeon was very matter of fact as he told us what he was up against, and he explained the surgery to the children. Several times he stressed the risks involved, but it was the only option for survival. The concern on Sam and Meg's faces turned to fear.

The more confident the surgeon seemed about the operation, the better I felt about it. I had no options, and I trusted God to bring me through this time just as He had so many times before. I also trusted Dr. Touloukian.

"Have the gates of death been shown to you? Have you seen the gates of the shadow of death? Have you comprehended the vast expanses of the earth? Tell me, if you know all this" (Job 38:17-18).

Now God is questioning Job and God is letting Job know that HE is the only one who dictates when our life is done. He determines our time of death, so who is Job to act as if he knows that he will die? God is in control as Job ponders his painful lot. When God is ready to take Job, then Job will die, but not until then. Only God is God, and we are not to act as if we have other knowledge.

"You will be secure, because there is hope; you will look about you and take your rest in safety" (Job 11:18).

In my case, I was shown a vision of heaven, but after that vision I did not die. God was in control, and He chose to honor the prayers of His people. So, that left me to believe I would not die any time soon. Dr. Touloukian painted a grim picture of a 50/50 chance of survival; however, God is God. He pulled me from the clutches of death time and time again, and I had no reason to believe this would be different. Only God would determine my time of death. God taught me an even greater faith in the midst of no hopeful signs. Yes, the surgery would be critical, but after all, He is God!

Chapter 39

Family Affair (January 2010, I.U. Medical Center)

The day of the surgery my entire family was there, once again, to support me. I was anxious about how all of this would turn out, but I was not scared of dying. I knew this was a very serious surgery; still I am a child of God, and I knew if I died I would be in heaven with Jesus. What I was afraid of was something going wrong, and I would possibly end up in a nursing home – that was not a pleasant thought.

After one of the residents approved their visit, the nurses reluctantly let my large family come back to see me, and I was so thankful for that, especially since about fifty family members filled my room. I was thrilled to see all of them, and I can't begin to express how precious my family is to me. Some chattered nervously, some remained silent, some cried, and I could see it was very difficult for my family to watch me go through this again. We have a shared love.

Suddenly, my family began to sing, and the music filled the room and spilled out into the hallway. Nurses peeked in to see where the beautiful music came from. My family sang in four part harmony, and it was the most wonderful sound I could imagine. It was just what I needed to soothe my weary soul, and after they sang a few songs, my family prayed. The Holy Spirit filled my room, and goose bumps erupted as several begged God to heal my body. We celebrated worship together!

Soon my family had to leave so I could be taken to surgery, and they headed to the waiting room. To my surprise, my family was just around the corner! When the nurses wheeled me out of my room and started down the long hallway to surgery, my family was lined up on both sides of the hallway all the way to the operating room. They smiled, cheered and waved me on, and it was as if I marched through a parade crowd. As I passed each person, hands from both sides reached to touch me, and kisses came from every direction. What a send-off!

God blessed me so much in those few brief moments, and I knew so many people would love to know this kind of love and support in a family. I praised God for the gift of my family, and a few days later I learned that while I was in surgery, a constant prayer vigil was kept in the chapel. My oldest sister, Sherry, has been a strong spiritual mentor for me, and we have encouraged each other in our faith. She organized the vigil where two family members at a time spent fifteen minutes in the chapel praying for me and Dr. Touloukian. When their fifteen minutes were up, two others continued in prayer. Just as the last two family members finished praying, the surgeon walked into the waiting room with the news, certifying God's impeccable timing.

I was informed that one of my cousins and her spouse were in the waiting room with my family the day of my surgery. As they left to go home, her husband turned to her and asked, "Where do you go to sign up to be a part of that family?" My family will never know the impact of their testimony in that waiting room. Many lives were touched that day – mine included.

Once I entered the operating room and the big double doors closed behind me, one of the nurses looked at me with the biggest smile and said, "You would think you were the President or something." The nurse was right, I felt that special! I know I didn't deserve all of this support, but I was sure grateful for it, and my family will never know the impact it made on me.

There on that cold metal table with that big round light hanging directly above me, I was calm, and I could feel myself relax as I had absolutely no fear. The anesthesiologist rubbed my hand and whispered in my ear, "Are you ready? It's no big deal. We do this everyday. Just kick back and take a little nap." I drifted off to sleep.

The surgery was a success! Praise God, He did another miracle! As an added blessing, removing the hernia allowed food and drink to flow into a very small section of colon that was not previously used. Now, I began to digest food better, and I absorbed more nutrients. In fact, I was getting enough fluids and nutrition that I no longer needed to have IV fluids infused at home. That was a huge gift! Praise the Lord!

"Where were you when I laid the earth's foundations? Tell me, if you understand" (Job 38:4).

God knows all my comings and goings, and He is aware of all that happens. Who am I to question His plans? Was all of this really even about me? I don't know. I know God will use anyone or anything to accomplish His plan. Maybe God used my adversities to work in the life of one of the people I encountered during my medical care. Was it a doctor, a family member, a nurse, an office worker, or a roommate? Surely it was not all about me. I was so confused, and I was beyond understanding who, what, why, when, or where. I reached a point of absolute peace with whatever the reason might be. If it was about me, I thanked God for working in my life so I might become the Christian He wants me to be. If it was about someone else, I thanked God for using me to fulfill His plan.

Chapter 40

God is Good All the Time (2006 to Present)

I have faced numerous challenges in my life. It has been a very hard life for me at times, but it has been filled with blessings and miracles that I could never imagine would happen. I should have been dead many times over, and there were serious complications too numerous to recall. I was angry at times, but I never once hated God or blamed Him for my illness.

I've had so many physical, spiritual, and emotional issues to deal with, but God did not leave me helpless or alone. He provided the most wonderful doctors, surgeons, and specialists over the course of the past six years. However, two special physicians remain close to my heart. My surgeon, Dr. Christopher Touloukian, and my family doctor, Dr. Mary McCullough, have been instrumental in my care and healing process. Dr. McCullough has never wavered in her support for me, and she has provided excellent care. She is a dear friend, and her staunch candidness makes me love her all the more. I am so thankful for her and for Dr. Touloukian!

Still, I am human. I have been scared, I've had lots of pain, and I have been extremely frustrated. My life as I once knew it is over, but I've learned a whole new way of life. When I was discouraged, God sent someone to refresh my soul and remind me that He is right there every minute and every second. I clung to His promises and I prayed intently for healing. From the point of absolute despair, many times I was lifted to the highest places where God's amazing gifts of charity, love, and mercy poured over me. I rode a physical and emotional roller coaster, but I continued to praise Him for all He brought me through.

My church and work families were there through it all, and they were literally the hands and feet of Christ. They blessed me in ways I never thought possible. From cooking to cleaning, visiting, baskets full of goodies, many prayers and much more, I am just amazed at the love showered over me and my family. We are also forever grateful to all those who left food on our porch and money in our mail box. We have no idea who those people are, but we love and appreciate all they have done for us. What a tremendous blessing they have been to us, and we are forever thankful!

My mother, Theresa C. Wenning, has been gone now for eighteen years and my dad, Donald H. Wenning, has been gone eight years. They both died from cancer, and I miss my parents terribly, but in their absence my siblings have filled a void only they could. God has used them to minister to me and to love me through the many difficult times I have faced in my journey. The countless hours I spent with my siblings as they cared for me were priceless. They talked with me into the wee hours of the morning until I could fall asleep. I was blessed with twelve brothers and sisters: Sherry, Mary, Dan, Mike, Paul, John, Nancy, Tina, Anna, Bill, Brian and Jim. They are listed from oldest to youngest, and I fall in line between Tina and Anna.

All of my brothers and sisters in-law were just as encouraging and loving towards me as my own siblings. Karl, Paul, Deanna, Sandy, Sue, Rachel, Larry, Dave, Scott, Julie, Patti and Gloria also took turns staying with me and showering me with love. I hesitate to call them in-laws because they are so dear to me. I love them as my own brothers and sisters! Every member of my family has been crucial in my recovery. God is still using them today, and I continue to be forever blessed and grateful for each one of them. God began a process in our family that took us all completely out of our comfort zones and challenged us to grow in Him as we never had before. God is so ... GOOD!

Larry's family was with their ailing mother, Lois. When they could do so, Larry's dad, Richard, five siblings, Pat, Sandy, Janet, Ronnie and Bill, as well as two brothers-in-law, Butch (Ron) and Todd, were there for me, too. They all struggled with wanting to be with their mother, but desired me to know they truly cared about me as well. If anyone understood, I did, and the feeling was mutual.

Lois wanted nothing more than to see all of her family come to know Jesus Christ as their Lord and Savior before she died. God used Lois and the beautiful witness she was for Him, even in death, to reach out to her family members for Him. I know that in her last days she touched each heart in such a way no one could deny her love for them or for Christ. I am so thankful I have been privileged to be a part of Larry's family. I love them very much!

Prayers have circulated throughout the country. From my first surgery, and still today, so many people pray for me and my family, and I'm sure I will never know the magnitude of prayer and its far-reaching hands. Larry and I are so thankful for every single prayer! Prayer definitely works, and we know how it touches the very heart of God. Larry, Sam, Megan and I want to express our heartfelt THANKS!

Someone asked me once, "What is it about you? Why have you 'monopolized' our church so?" The question surprised me. If my situation touched the hearts of literally hundreds of people and caused them to pray for God's healing in my life, then I would gladly monopolize the church. At the very least, it encouraged people to get down on their knees and talk to God. In that, God is glorified. So, I guess it's all GOOD!

If the concern was that I somehow prevented a whole church from worshiping God because the members were so focused on me and my illness, be assured that was not the case. Our church did and still does care deeply for all our members. We love one another, and we pray for every member who is in need with the same earnest desire to see God meet that individual's need. We have also been very active in projects and events that have helped many members in their time of need, and in all of it God was glorified. So, again, I guess it's all still GOOD!

We never know whom God will use or how He will use us to accomplish His will. When we allow ourselves to be willing vessels for God, we must accept all that comes with it. It might mean we encounter hardship, or we may have to sacrifice something. To be used requires our action, and when we allow God to use us we may or may not fully understand the good that will come of it – the good for God and for His people. Victim or vessel? I choose vessel.

My plea is that God is glorified in all my words and actions. I pray those reading this will understand that, as have I, their only hope is in Jesus Christ!

Chapter 41

Life Today (Present Day)

Today, life is much different. I almost said much better, but that is not true. During the time of my most horrendous pain and suffering, I was also at my time of most incredible growth and renewal. My soul cried out, and God heard my cries – He sustained me through it all. He was, and is, my rock and my salvation. To Him be all glory and praise!

Yes, today life is different and it's good. I am doing far better than I was six years ago, but my physical condition changes from day to day. I am trying to walk a little each day, and at times, I am able to walk up to three miles. I really enjoy walking outside! I continue to face many challenges, and my energy level bounces up and down like a yo-yo. I live one day at a time, and sometimes I live one second at a time. Larry and I still struggle financially, and when my physical condition is a mess, it seems my emotions follow suit.

Spiritually, I am growing closer to Jesus every day. I am certainly not Job, but I have come through some really difficult struggles, and have become a far better child and servant of God. What's important is that I am alive, I serve a risen Savior, and I am continually blessed with His sweet refreshment. Every negative in my life God has used for good. How can I not praise Him? Thank You, dear God, for all You have done for me!

Both of my children have graduated from college. Meg is a registered nurse and Sam is a personal trainer. They are very independent and responsible adults, and I could not be more proud of them or love them more. They both love Jesus, and that is a blessing to me. I can't imagine life without Megan and Sam, and I am so thankful for every moment I am privileged to be their mother.

My husband is one extraordinary man, and I mean that with all my heart! Larry loves God and is a great source of spiritual strength for me, and together we seek refuge in God. Larry is incredibly strong, but he is also very tender-hearted. When I'm sick, or have a colostomy accident, Larry is so calm and loving. He helps me clean up, cries with me, and then we laugh together until we can't laugh anymore. Larry never remarks about the ugly scars that cover the entire trunk of my body, or complains about the bags and bandages that cover and hang from my abdomen. He never remarks about how my body has aged or how the lack of nutrition has damaged my hair and skin. Larry always tells me he loves me and that I am beautiful. He touches me and caresses me when I can't even look at myself. I don't believe any other man would endure all that he has these past six years and remained with me as he has. He is my best friend and I love him with all my heart! Every day I pray for him and thank God for him. Thank You, dear Lord, for my precious Larry.

Chapter 42

Final Thoughts (Present Day)

My trials are no comparison to what Job endured. Likewise, my trials and tribulations will never compare to what Jesus Christ endured for me. Jesus is perfect and sinless, yet Jesus, in His innocence, was tortured and crucified. He could have condemned me to hell, but He has given me mercy instead. He chose to go to the cross, and He has granted me grace. His ultimate sacrifice for the forgiveness of sin proves Jesus defeated death on the cross, and He has transferred the gift of salvation to me. Because no one understands more than Jesus what I have been through and how I will continue to face challenges, I will forever be indebted to Him, and my desire is that my life glorifies Him.

Thank you, readers, for sharing in this journey with me. I pray you have found a precious nugget of truth that will help you in your own journey, and that you have been inspired to deepen your walk with Christ. I pray you know that the problems you are facing can be a blessing in your life, too. May you find comfort and peace in knowing that you CAN endure and overcome adversities with God's help!

If you are reading this book, and you do not have a personal relationship with Jesus, you can do that today. God loves you so much, and He wants you to spend eternity in heaven with Him. There IS a literal heaven and hell, so please do not wait until it's too late. Listen to the call of Jesus and invite Him into your heart today.

I have listed some Scriptures that will be helpful in understanding God's love and how you can have a personal relationship with Him now.

"For God so loved the world that he gave his one and only Son, that whoever believes in him shall not perish but have eternal life" (John 3:16).

"There is no one righteous ..." (Romans 3:10).

... all have sinned and fall short of the glory of God (Romans 3:23).

For the wages of sin is death, but the gift of God is eternal life ... (Romans 6:23).

... While we were still sinners, Christ died for us (Romans 5:8).

That if you confess with your mouth, "Jesus is Lord," and believe in your heart that God raised him from the dead, you will be saved. For it is with your heart that you believe and are justified and it is with your mouth that you confess and are saved (Romans 10:9-10).

"... Everyone who calls on the name of the Lord will be saved" (Romans 10:13).

... believe in the name of the Son of God so that you may know that you have eternal life (1 John 5:13).

Jesus is standing at the door knocking. He wants to come into your heart *(Revelation 3:20).*

Receiving Jesus is simply a matter of asking Him to come into your heart and life, asking Him to forgive your sins, and asking Him to become your Lord and Savior. It is an act of sincere faith and an honest desire to give God complete control of your life. You can receive Jesus as your personal Lord and Savior right now if you choose to do so.

Below is a prayer, a guideline that you can use to pray to accept God's gift of salvation:

"Father, I know that I have sinned, and my sins have separated me from You. I am truly sorry, and I need forgiveness of my sin.

Please forgive me, and help me to avoid sinning again. God, I believe that Your Son, Jesus Christ, died for my sins, He was resurrected from the dead, He is alive, and He hears my prayer. Please Jesus, come into my heart and become the Lord and Savior of my life. I want You to reign in my heart forever. Please send Your Holy Spirit to help me to remain faithful to You, and to do Your will for the rest of my life. In Jesus' name I pray, Amen."

If you said this prayer and accepted Jesus Christ as your personal Lord and Savior, congratulations! Welcome to the Family of God!

The Bible tells us to follow up on our commitment. It is important to be baptized as Christ commanded.

> *"... Repent and be baptized, every one of you, in the name of Jesus Christ for the forgiveness of your sins. And you will receive the gift of the Holy Spirit" (Acts 2:38).*

I am so excited for you! Please share your decision with your pastor or minister so your church family can rejoice with you, and they can help you to begin your new journey with Jesus. Your pastor can also help you in your decision to be baptized.

If you do not belong to a church, seek fellowship with other Christians. Find a local church to worship God and grow in your new relationship with Jesus. Remember to share your decision with your new minister.

Finally, please remember that Christianity is not a religion; it is a relationship – a relationship with Jesus Christ. Please do not neglect this new relationship with Christ, as it is the single most important decision you will ever make. It is important that you read your Bible. There is so much for you to learn about our Awesome God, and the Bible is His love letter to us. Reading your Bible will help you to grow and develop into the man or woman of God that He has created you to be!

God Bless You Always,

Debbie

Order Form

Please feel free to copy this form for your order.

You may contact the author by email at:

ldthomas82@hotmail.com

To order individual copies directly from the author,
mail a copy of this form and your payment to:

Debbie Thomas
P.O. Box 127
Greensburg, IN 47240

From Pain to Peace - **$14.95** plus shipping

Quantity _____ @ $14.95 each....................... $_____

7% Sales Tax (IN residents only - $1.05/copy) .. $_____

Shipping ($5.00/copy)... $_____

TOTAL... $_____

Send To:

NAME_____

ADDRESS_____

CITY_____STATE_____ZIP_____

PHONE_____

EMAIL_____